MEMO

UN
TORTURED
ROMANS 8:1

SHERRY WALKER

DEDICATION

Father God, all the glory and praise belongs to you!

Father God, I pray for your children that are oppressed and dealing with their past will receive your love, grace, and mercy and know that Jesus died for us. Thank you for giving me to my biological daddy and then transferring me to my spiritual Father and being present with me the whole time! In my Lord and Savior's name, Jesus the Christ.

-

This book is dedicated to my daddy, Mr. Carroll Edward Walker Sr. He was the only man I thought could ever love me the way that I am and love me through everything. Daddy, you are truly missed here on earth. The greatest and first love for me was to know that my daddy truly loved me. Daddy, you were truly the best dad ever to me, but to find out our Heavenly Father is the best of them all is amazing!

ACKNOWLEDGEMENTS

To my mother Priscilla Mae, I love you so much. You made many sacrifices for our family. I want to thank you personally and publicly for all that you have done and continue to do for me. I couldn't ask God for a better mother who birthed and took care of me. You have always loved me even when I didn't understand the tough love you gave me. Mama you are the best! I love you.

-

To my husband Franklin Anthony, thank you for truly understanding why this book had to written. Thank you for loving me through my flaws, baggage, faults, and whatever else life threw our way. In spite of the craziness, you endured with me...you stayed. Your willingness to love my whole package, stepping in and stepping up to help me raised my daughter as your own has truly blessed my life. You are one special guy! I love baby!

-

To my daughter Dominique, I love you so much. My baby my gift from God, words cannot express how I'm so grateful you chose to unconditionally love me and your father in spite of our past. I knew while you were in my womb that you were going to be a fighter. Thank you for all you have done in honoring me and both of your dads. You are truly an amazing woman. Your heart is priceless. Continue to share your heart with the world. I'm so proud to be your mom.

-

To my god-mother Mrs. Linda Eady and my daughter's god-mother Mrs. Pearl Forbes, may you two continue to rest in Heaven. I thank you both from my heart, all that you have done for my daughter and me. It truly takes a village to raise a child. I thank God that He had you two in mind to be a part of our village.

-

To my Aunt Pookie, you already know you are my girl! I love you so much. Your love, laughter, and encouragement has always played a part in my life. Thank you as well for helping me to find my way and giving me a chance to get on my feet during a hard time in my life.

-

To my God Sister Maxine Plater, thanks for being an encouragement in my life and always reminding me about how much I have inspired you to not give up on your dreams by sharing my dream with you. Love you dearly.

-

To Asia and Tamara, my stylists, and friends, you have encouraged me, cried with me, prayed with me while this book was being written. It didn't matter that I was older than you two, the wisdom that God poured out of you into my life was priceless. You are truly anointed with gifted hands.

-

To my BG Family! The Butler Garden's Crew from up the hill to down the hill, I had the best childhood life with you guys! Living in that 12-building complex along with red brick buildings at the front of 16th & Butler Street, SE was family! You guys are always in my heart! Thanks for sharing your parents, siblings, children, pets, and whatever else you had that I needed.

-

To my prayer line sisters! Every Saturday morning at 7:00 for the last two years, we came together and prayed for others, creating a safe place to lay down our hearts, love, and have compassion for others. Thank you all for praying for me, encouraging me, and reminding me how much God loves and hears us.

To my WWW staff sisters-in-Christ, serving our 1st Lady together has been nothing but a blessing to me. Women coming together in prayer, love, and compassion for other women has truly blessed my life. Many days I felt beat up by life but coming to serve in ministry with you ladies my strength was renewed from all the sincere hugs, prayers, and working together. I love all of you.

-

To Minister Pamela Price, thank you for the impartation and the spoken word God released in my life through you, that I was good enough no matter how times I was overlooked. You had to stand on your tippy toes to anoint my head. I love you dearly. I'll never forget your labor of love.

-

To the SOFCC pastoral staff, thank you for the heartfelt Bible study teachings that impacted my life. Thank you to the youth department for embracing and helping me with my daughter in the beginning.

-

Lastly to my Pastors Apostles Michael & Dee Dee Freeman of Spirit of Faith Christian Center, I came to your ministry a broken woman covered in designer labels to camouflage my pain. Your love and hearts to accept the rejected is amazing. Before I really knew how much God loved me, He showed me through you. I thank you for loving God's chosen people and truly being an example of what you heard and preached from God for His Children. I have been under your leadership for the last 21 years and my life and family have grown tremendously in love and unity. Restored family relationships have come out of you showing love and acceptance towards me during some of the most devastating times in my life. Agape love, forgiveness, faith, family, finances and now fitness, has been at the forefront in your ministry. May God bless you always.

DISCLAIMER

Un-tortured: Romans 8:1 is my written testimony. This book is about my experiences and actions as I began to follow God's instructions. I am a Christian. It is a work of creative fiction. The words are mine alone and are not intended to hurt anyone. The events are depicted to the best of my memory and the stories in this book are true. However, identifying details have been omitted to protect the privacy of those involved. The dialogue in this book comes from my recollections and is not written to represent word-for-word conversations. In all instances, the spirit of the dialogue is accurate. This book is not intended to be anything more than a creative work of literature.

FOREWORD

It's an honor to know my daughter Sherry has embraced her identity in me. I knew when I knitted her in her mother's womb that she would be more than a conquer. Sherry is fearfully and wonderfully made. Even though Sherry has not seen my Son who paid the price for her life, she believes in Him and is blessed. Sherry knows how to cast her cares onto Me, and I will sustain her. I comfort Sherry and have compassion on her. Sherry's broken heart is healed, and her wounds are bound up. I have not given Sherry the spirit of fear but of power and of love and of a sound mind. Sherry is strong and courageous. She doesn't have to be afraid or discourage for I'm with her wherever she goes. Sherry has my faithful love and mercies afresh each morning. I will keep Sherry strong to the end so that she will be free from blame on the day when her Lord and Savior Jesus the Christ returns. My Son poured out His blood of the covenant for forgiveness of Sherry's sins. Even when Sherry went astray, I showed her the proper path to take. Because Sherry's hope is in me, I always renew her strength and she soars on wings like an eagle, she will run and not go weary, and she will walk and not be faint. My joy is Sherry's strength. Sherry rejoices because her name is written in heaven.

Who is forwarding this book? Sherry's Heavenly Father! God is Who I Am!

"By faith, my daughters and sons, before you move forward in this book, know that my words apply to you as well. Walk in my grace, mercy, and forgiveness in spite of your past through my son Jesus the Christ."

INTRODUCTION

God placed this book in my heart back in 2015, in a dramatically artistic form. I envisioned creating a large heavy blanket with lots of soft mannequin wig heads. Each head represented the torturing thoughts in my mind that had me bound. I didn't want to write my thoughts or my vision because I wasn't ready to share my truth. I did create the thoughts on the mannequin head. Then God reminded me about the threats I made to my little cousins when we were young. I used to threaten one of my little cousins by telling her she wasn't my cousin anymore whenever I was mad at her. She cried and begged me to let her be my cousin. I let it go on for hours before telling her she could be my cousin again. She had no clue that I didn't have the power to take that position away from her.

I had another cousin who at the time was three years old. He didn't like for anyone to dare him to do or not to do something. I dared him sometimes, just because I knew he didn't like it and it would make him mad. One time, I double-D dared him to give me his candy.

He got mad and cried, "You better not dare me because I will do it. I will give you all of my candy!"

He was a child and had no clue that I was tricking him out of his candy. He also had little action figurines that he loved. When one went missing, he went off. He didn't care if that one figurine had a broken leg or arm. Even when the head was missing, he wanted his figurine back. Until we found that figurine, he didn't rest. He went to sleep crying and woke up crying for his figurine. That little three-year-old didn't want a new one, even when he was promised to get several new figurines. We looked everywhere for that broken figurine. Once it was found, we had to immediately get it to him. Back then, we didn't have a car, so it required someone to take the bus to return his figurine to him. God is the same way about us. He still wants his children. God began to share with me that the devil was doing to me the things I had done to my little cousins.

The devil was tricking me with fear. I was afraid to write this book, and the devil was using fear and tortured thoughts to make me believe that I wasn't accepted in the beloved and my story didn't matter. The devil had me believing that people would taunt and laugh at me. The devil threatened my livelihood if this book came out. The devil double-d dared me to release this book. The devil said that no one will forward this book. My mind was reeling, and I was living in darkness and constantly tortured by negative thoughts embedded in my mind by the devil. Finally, I remembered who I am—God's child! I began to fight to get out of the darkness and free from the devil's torture. I am a child of God, and the devil has no power to cancel the blood of Jesus for my shame, pain, and sins.

You may be broken, depressed, abused, grief ridden, or dealing with shame from your past, but God still loves and wants you. It doesn't matter who threw you away or your past, God still wants you. The devil has no right to take away the purpose and plan God has for your life.

God said, "Write the book!"

After a few years, I started a new job. On my first day at work, I got off the elevator and walked into my first coworker. I introduced myself as the new employee. When my new coworker looked at me, she was sobbing, and her blouse was a little wet from the tears rolling down her face. She was uncontrollably crying. She proceeded to tell me she lost her father a year ago and the pain of his death still hurt. She said the grief gets so unbearable at times as if it just happened. I grieved for five years over my dad. I began to share with her how I overcame my grief of losing my dad. Towards the end of my first week, I walked around the office to familiarize myself with my new surroundings. One of my co-workers complimented me on my lipstick. We began to talk, and I noticed she wasn't wearing makeup. She stated that she couldn't wear lipstick. I asked why, and she said that her ex-husband, noticed I said ex-husband, told her she looked like a clown in makeup. For years, I was stuck by the evil things spoken to me by my ex-boyfriend. I asked why she was still letting her ex-husband control her life. I told her she had beautiful lips and to go buy some lipstick. Her eyes filled with tears, and she began to cry. The next week she came to work with beautiful red lipstick on and showed me a picture she had taken over the weekend. She wore a beautiful black dress with her new lipstick.

After a few months, I began to have a conversation with a beautiful woman in a high-ranking position. She was a Christian. It looked like she had it all together. I couldn't shake off what she shared with me. I was also stuck where she continues to be. I was in the same place for 20 years and now I'm out of it.

God began to speak to me, and He said, "These episodes are the reason I need you to share your story.

You are not the only one the devil attacks. Many of my sons and daughters need to be free. Write the book!"

In 1998, I rededicated my life to God. I truly knew in my heart that was what I needed and more than anything, wanted in my life. I was stuck, stuck, stuck in my mind that I didn't deserve it. I believed that God didn't love me, couldn't and wouldn't use me for anything. My thoughts tortured me for years, every day, all day long, and every time I thought about God's love for me. I was basing His love for me on my ability to love myself. I was trying to love myself by doing good works, which didn't happen. I kept trying to serve in ministry, give my time, talents, and offerings, and just being a good human being. It felt good, but then torturous thoughts in my mind crushed every effort to feel loved by God. I couldn't continue in my own strength. I was no match for the devil.

Once I realized I wasn't moving forward and kept reliving the pain and shame, I had to go back and completely dig up the roots. I had to own my mistakes and faults. I had to face my pain and shame. I had to release those who tortured me in any way. Most importantly, I had to walk by faith and receive every promise from God through Jesus. I had to learn how to receive, depend on, and confess Philippians 4:13: "I can do all things through

Christ which strengthens me." I also had to believe, receive, and confess Romans 8:1: "There is therefore now no condemnation to those who are in Christ Jesus, who do not walk according to the flesh, but according to the Spirit." Jesus was the answer I needed. He finished everything pertaining to life and Godliness. 2 Peter 1:3 (KJV) states, "According as his divine power hath given unto us all things that pertain unto life and godliness, through the knowledge of Him that hath called us to glory and virtue." My heavenly Father shared with me that so many of his sons and daughters are *stuck* in their minds, just as I was being tortured every second of everyday, hearing the lies of the enemy. The devil is the accuser of the brethren. The devil uses half-truths to torture the mind. The devil will constantly use your past against you when you don't renew your mind. The Bible tells the believer to renew our minds. This responsibility was given to the believer. Romans 12:2 says, "And be not conformed to this world: but be ye transformed by the renewing of you mind, that ye may prove what is that good, and acceptable, and perfect, will of God." You must renew your mind! How? With the Word of God daily!

God instructed His children to take every thought captive as in 2 Corinthians 10:5 (NKJV) by casting down arguments and every high thing that exalts itself against the knowledge of God, bringing every thought into captivity to the obedience of Christ. The devil will constantly use your mind as his playground to defeat you. The devil only knows your past. Only God knows our end from the beginning. Everything in the middle God knew about beforehand. God knew about everything that would take place in your life. Jeremiah 29:11 (KJV) states, "For I know the thoughts that I think toward you, saith the Lord, thoughts of peace, and not of evil, to give you an expected end." From the beginning, God gave us an expected end. Most believers in the body of Christ have masked their secrets, deadly strongholds, in their lives and are afraid to share what is really holding them back from believing and receiving all that God has for them. Suicide is the deception which the devil is slowly using against the God head. God's Word is our defense attorney, healer, promise keeper, friend, and all! Jesus paid the ultimate price for everyone. We only needed to receive Him! It wasn't based on our ability to save ourselves.

Jesus Christ is the best gift I have ever received, lasting throughout eternity. Finding out who my heavenly Father is, receiving the Holy Spirit, and finding out all that was paid in full for my life and given to me is amazing. I am on a new journey! Getting to know my heavenly Father through his Word, but first finding out how much He loves me and has loved me through every torturing thought and pain is incredible. Knowing that there is nothing I have done or what has been done to me that His love can't cover through the blood of Jesus!

CONTENTS

REMEMBERING THE GRIEF AND LOVE

Chapter 1

THE CALL

It was a wonderful spring day on Friday, April 14, 1995. I went to work as scheduled from 12:00 pm until 9:00 pm. My dad and I planned to go out of town after I got off from work to attend my great-grandmother's funeral the next day. My dad called my job at 7:30 pm to ask if we were still leaving when I got off.

"Daddy, I'm really tired and I don't think I will be able to drive so late."

He was always understanding. Dad stated that he was still leaving in the morning to attend the funeral.

He said, "Baby girl, I need some money to get a haircut."

"Daddy, call me in the morning."

"Okay baby, bye baby."

"I felt something when my daddy said, 'Bye baby,'" I shared with my co-worker.

I tried to call back. I called the operator. I needed to get him back on the phone. With no luck, I couldn't retrieve a call back number because I was using a business line. When my dad spoke to me, he was always soft spoken. The "bye baby" was quieter than his normal voice. I could not shake the feeling I had. It was not normal, and I was troubled. I completed my shift, went to pick up my daughter, and headed home for the night.

While growing up, my dad told his children that whenever we are in the bed for the night, never ever let anyone take us out of it.

He said, "It's not a good thing to do."

He meant that we might not return or something bad could happen. It truly had to be a life-or-death situation.

I received a phone call from my sister Carolyn around 11:30 pm. She wanted me to bring my daughter to our mother's home to be with my baby nephew Brian because he wasn't used to her keeping him. My daughter was the only one who could help Carolyn to calm and stop him from crying. We jumped in the car headed to my mom's house and then I returned home alone to sleep.

On April 15, 1995, my life changed forever! Around 1:30 in the morning, I got the call. Yes me. The caller on the other end was my Aunt Ella.

She asked, "How are you?

"I'm okay."

I was so glad to hear her voice, I hadn't seen or heard from her in a couple of years.

"Who's with you?"

"Nobody," I answered.

"Are you sitting down?"

"Yes."

Then the unthinkable was said to me. My daddy was dead!

"Dead! Who killed my dad?"

He was not into anything for someone would want to harm him. My dad was doing okay. He had two mild back-to-back heart attacks at the end 1994, which at the time, we weren't scared because he was being released when we arrived at hospital. On April 15, 1995, my dad had a massive heart attack at the poker table while at a friend's house. He died doing what he loved.

I had to call to my sister Carolyn and my brother Carroll Jr. I left my sister and brother at my mother's house just two hours before.

Angry, my sister answered the phone and yelled, "Who the hell calling here this late?"

With a cracking voice and tears rolling down my face, I called her name three times before she realized it was me. I asked her to tell my oldest brother to pick up the phone in the other room. I only wanted to say it once. Carolyn screamed. She had to catch her breath. It was painful to hear. I went back to my mom's house so that we could go the hospital. My sister-in-love Cheryl was there to take care of the children while we set out to the hospital. Before leaving, I needed to hear from my mama. At the time, she was out of town at the celebration of life for my great-grandma Miss Lizzie. My mother and father were no longer married but they were best friends. I knew they still loved each other. My mama said a few words and I knew her heart was broken. She sensed that I was in bad shape. My daddy was everything to me.

While riding to Howard University Hospital in Washington, D.C., tears rolled down our faces. We were in complete disbelief. We hoped it was not true. We arrived and our younger brother met us at the car. We went in together, still hoping to see our daddy alive.

The nurse handed me my daddy's driver's license. I knew it was true. I wanted to see him in a hospital bed so that I could awaken him, not in the freezer at the morgue. The drawer was pulled out and he was lifeless. I was given a plastic bag that contained his ripped clothing. What was the point of giving them to me? I still have his sneakers in my closet. Because it seemed unreal, I went back later in the morning to see him again. The nurse advised me not to, but I had to see him. My heart shattered into a thousand pieces. How was I going to live without my daddy? I thought about him dying in my car had we been on the road at the time of his death. It hurt. For years afterward, repeatedly, the thought crossed my mind. I felt tortured. It didn't happen, yet I couldn't get it out of my mind.

Going to the hospital to break the news to my sister Vanessa with my mother was beyond devastating because she loved our daddy even the more. She wondered why so many of our family members were visiting my mom's home days before. No one was allowed to mention the news about my dad to her over the phone. While my mom spoke with her doctors to prepare to break the news to her about our dad, I was in the waiting area. When Vanessa saw me, she couldn't believe I was there to see her. She had been in the hospital on and off for several years, but I didn't go to see her.

"Why you are here?" she questioned.

She reminded me that I hadn't come to see her. I felt like a water balloon, overflowing with tears ready to burst. I couldn't hold it. While walking behind her on the way to conference room the tears flowed like a river. The news was given to her. She screamed but then her focus was on me. She knew I was in bad shape. She felt so sorry for me, and the hug she gave me was priceless. I gave her a picture of our dad to keep. She attended the wake but not the funeral because it was out of town.

Planning the funeral was easy for me, but it was hard for my sister Carolyn. She was the oldest and planning events was instilled in her when she was young. Carolyn was prepared to take on the expenses because she had an insurance policy. I helped with selecting his clothing, the funeral home, and a casket. His suit and casket were gray, my daddy's favorite color. Our mom was by our side. She made sure that we purchased underwear, a tee shirt, and socks for him. The funeral home director said we didn't need those items, but mom said that we did. He was fully dressed! I was excited, but unsure why.

His family came together to celebrate his life. At the wake, I saw many of his friends that I hadn't seen since I was a little girl. The wake was packed. I was happy and didn't know why. When it was time to shut the casket, my happiness ended.

As his younger brothers were closing his casket, I asked my Uncle Darryl, "Why are you closing his casket?"

Uncle Darryl didn't sugar-coat anything, he answered, "I'm driving my big brother home."

"You not scared to drive my dad tonight down home for that long ride?"

"What you think he is going to do...get up and start talking again!"

Uncle Jerome on the other hand hugged me and said, "It's going to be alright. We got him."

As tears welled, I was happy to see my dad's baby brothers take him home until the funeral, which was to be held in two days.

The day before the celebration, I went to see my daddy. To my surprise, the funeral home in Franklin, Virginia was open to the public. A guy was standing at his casket. I stood back to let him have his moment. The man was quite upset, and he kept shaking his head and saying that he couldn't believe it. He began to bang on the casket. I went up to console him. I asked him how he knew my dad.

He responded, "I don't. I just come in here every day to see who is in here."

I said some unhealthy things to that idiot. Today I can laugh about it. Then I was hurt. He was lucky I was the only one in my family who witnessed what he had done.

As a child in the summertime, my friends and I went to the neighborhood funeral home to visit people's wake. We viewed the body, talked to the families, told stories as if we knew the person, and even consumed some of the refreshments. One day, a lady was happy because her elderly mother was loved by us. We lied about how her mom gave us candy and let us in her house. Complete lies. I didn't know that one day I was going to reap what I sowed. The bible clearly states in Galatians 6:7 (NKJV), "Do not be deceived, God is not mocked; for whatever a man sows, that he will also reap."

When my daddy's casket was being closed, a woman snatched the pillow from under his head, causing his head to turn. Even though he was dead, I felt like she broke his neck. She then threw the pillow on top of him and closed the casket. It hurt so bad to see that! I couldn't speak. I hollered in despair. I jumped over the pew to get to him. Everyone thought I lost it. Years later, at my uncle's burial site, she was stung by a bee and had to be rushed to the hospital! I was happy and laughed! It was payback for what she did to my daddy!

Five years afterwards, my heart was still broken. I was drowning in grief and despair. He was buried four hours away from Maryland where I lived. I attempted to drive at least twice during the week to visit his gravesite. Some days I just drove and cried for hours. No one knew why I abruptly left work. Although I was tired and worn out from driving so much, I had to keep my promise to visit. I didn't tell my boyfriend at the time what I was doing. I made it home before my normal shift ended—when I was expected. He drove me down on weekends, and that was my reason for keeping quiet.

Grief, overwhelming grief, is what I had. It was so bad that I wanted to dig up my daddy, put him in my car, and bring him back home with me. The December after his death, the first snow fell. It was a blizzard in Maryland. I called my Uncle Jerome around midnight. Crying, I asked if it was snowing down there.

He replied, "Yes baby."

I wanted him to take a blanket to my daddy so that he wouldn't be cold.

"Baby, he's alright. He can't feel the snow. He's in a vault and he's alright," he answered.

"Are you sure?

I had it bad.

My tears flowed non-stop. I couldn't see. My heart ached. I couldn't control my feelings. I wanted my daddy back! One evening while driving home from work, one of his favorite songs was played on the radio. It was "Love Don't Love Nobody" by the Spinners. I lost it. My heart ached and I had to pull over. I should have turned to a different station, but I believed that my dad wanted me to hear the song. When I was a little girl, I sat with him and listened to oldies-but-goodies. At that moment, he was with me. Tears flowed. I needed my daddy. I wanted my daddy back. I missed my daddy.

On April 15th every year, I could not keep control. All I could think about was the day my daddy left. I kept relieving the day of his death all day. My tears were non-stop. I sat and stared at the pictures I took of him in the casket and cried for hours. I was angry with so many people because I felt they didn't care that my daddy was no longer here and should be still hurting because of my daddy's death like I hurt. No one loved him like I did. The only way I felt like I could get over my daddy's death was to die and be with him. Nothing and no one else mattered to me. I was ready to end my life.

Chapter 2

WHY MY DADDY MEANT SO MUCH TO ME

I wanted to know more about myself. I was the fourth child out of five children...the baby girl. The best place to get that information from was the woman who birthed me. I wanted to know about my first day on planet earth. I was born at home, assisted by a midwife, in Newsoms Virginia. My mother explained that they didn't think I was going to live because I weighed just under two pounds. My mother was sickly but carried me for nine months. Satan was after me from the beginning. My parents didn't take me to the hospital. They took care of me. I was amazed upon learning about it. Most babies that tiny were kept in an incubator. Because I was so small, my daddy carried me around on a pillow. My mom told me that a little girl thought I was a doll baby and almost snatched me off the pillow. My daddy saved me! I felt so special when she shared the story with me. Because my daddy was protective, no one could touch me. Now, I know that God's protection for me, as it is stated in Psalm 91.

I wanted to know how I got my nickname. My daddy came home from work one day, took off his work boots, and placed me in one of his boots. When I began to walk, I was still tiny. I walked under the dining table without bumping my head. My daddy gave me my nickname Boodie.

My daddy was everything to me. He kissed me in the middle of my forehead all the time. Those kisses were heartfelt. He often sat in the living room to watch television—five of them. One was a color floor model, and the others were smaller black and white, all on top of the floor model. My daddy didn't miss a thing. When I came into the living room and gave him my doll babies to keep while I pretended to go to the store, he fell asleep with them in his arm. My daddy let me plait his hair and put my barrettes on the ends to keep his curly hair from loosening. Sometimes he went to work without removing them. My daddy loved being around me and it showed. Jesus loved being around children in bible. Jesus took time with the children as well. Matthew 19:13-14 (KJV) reads, "Then little children were brought to Him that He might put His hands on them and pray, but the disciples rebuked them. But Jesus said, 'Let the little children come to Me, and do not forbid them; for of such is the kingdom of heaven.' And he laid his hands on them, and departed thence." My daddy ate with me during teatime using my tea set.

My dad only had an 8th grade education and was a hard worker. He was the best garage man who worked in the United States! His job didn't require a high school diploma but wanted a dedicated person. When I was a little girl, I was ashamed to say that he was a garbage man. One day, he found a brand-new doll with all the accessories at work and brought it home just for me. My friends wanted him to find them one too. People now see how great garbage men and environmental services workers are since they helped to preserve life during the viral pandemic.

He took me with him everywhere. When I was a little girl, we went out of town to visit family. It was late, and I was supposed to stay with them while daddy went out on the town for the night. I was not used to them. I cried and I didn't let go of my daddy. They tried to pull us apart, but I wouldn't let go. He knew I was afraid of them and carried me on his hip to a crap game. He played with me as he won big time. It may sound like a bad environment to take a child, but I felt safe with my daddy. I now have that same assurance that I'm safe with Father God and I have no fear. Isaiah 41:10 states, "Fear thou not; for I am with thee: be not dismayed; for I am thy God: I will strengthen thee; yea, I will help thee; yea, I will uphold thee with the right hand of my righteousness."

My daddy loved the Temptations. His favorite song by them was "My Baby!" We often danced to that song. I so love and miss my daddy. He protected me, even when I was wrong. When I was 11 years old, I committed a horrible act towards another child. My mom arrived home first and gave me whipping. When my daddy came home, before he could take off his shoes, my mom demanded that he whip me too.

He looked at me with compassion and asked my mom, "Didn't you already spank her?"

"Yes, and you need to do the same."

My dad took me into the room alone with a belt in his hand. He saw that I was still crying. He whispered in my ear and told me to cry loud as he hit the bed with the belt. At that moment, I believed I could be an actress. When he finished, he kissed my forehead. My daddy's compassion for me reminded me of the compassion the Lord has for mankind. In Psalm 145:8 (KJV), it states, "The LORD is gracious, and full of compassion; slow to anger, and of great mercy."

I was a mischievous little girl and often did things that was wrong toward others. I loved roses, and one day I picked all the roses off a tree in a lady's yard. She snitched.

I had the roses in my hand and hair. My dad listened to her complaint.

"They are not hers. They belong to the earth." I said,

My dad gave me kiss on my forehead and instructed me to stay out her yard. On another occasion, I sprayed ketchup and threw eggs at some neighbors out of anger. I had all the evidence on me. A parent came and informed my dad. Once again, he kissed my forehead and said not to waste food in that way. I wasn't given the punishment my mom and others thought I should have received from my daddy. Jesus took our punishment, can you relate? Those kisses on my forehead helped me not to commit those mistakes or acts again.

My dad truly loved everyone. I adored how he loved his brothers and sisters. The love my daddy had for his sibling was priceless. He showed me how to love my siblings even when they didn't do everything right. When I was young, one of his brother's pulled a gun on him. I was devastated to know my uncle did that. I was in tears and had nightmares. That uncle was one of my favorite uncles. My dad explained to me that on the day it happened, it wasn't his brother. It was a sickness my uncle was going through, and everything was alright. My dad went to see his brother the next day as if nothing happened. One of my uncles got into some trouble, and when my dad heard about it, he got dressed to see about him. My mom was against my dad leaving.

He said, "I love my brothers and sisters and I'm going to let my brother know he is not alone. I can't get him out of jail, but I'm going to let him see my face."

I learned that in the time of trouble, even when a person is wrong, your love for them shouldn't change. God promised to be with us in trouble. Psalm 46:1 (KJV) avows, "God is our refuge and strength, a very present help in trouble."

My dad made his nieces and nephews feel like they were his favorites. He looked out for his siblings and their children while still making sure that my siblings and I felt cared for and loved. After his death, I began to see my dad's heart and unconditional love as described in the Bible towards me. It seemed unreal. My dad wasn't a perfect man. He had his faults and shortcomings. One thing my dad did do right was that he loved me. After I walked away when I was a teenager and young adult to do life my way, he was there whenever I called him.

I took the time I had with my daddy for granted. I believed I would have him for a lifetime. I only had him for twenty-five years. I should have visited him more. I should have called more. I should have…I should have…is all I had left. Devastated, for five years I prayed for more time with daddy. While dealing with the grief, painful memories resurfaced that had nothing to do with grief. I thought I had healed from my past. One thing that brought me hope was to know my daddy accepted Jesus the Christ as his Lord and Savior. To find out in the Word of God that he would live in eternity...forever...was priceless! I will see him again!

Chapter 3

1999 – THE YEAR OF CHANGE

In March of 1998, I purchased my first house and joined a church. My daughter lived during the week with her godmother, who was my next-door neighbor, until she was in the third grade. She then lived with my mom until she began middle school. I was finally going to have her living with me again. I felt like my life began to change for the better. I was still grieving over my daddy, but I had something else to keep me moving forward. Upon joining the church, I wanted to know God and my Savior Jesus Christ. I was so consumed with church work and did not develop a relationship with God. I was new member and was immediately thrown into serving. I was asked to join two usher boards. I also had to pay dues. I didn't know what the dues were, but I was expected to pay them right away. I experienced love when I put on the usher uniform and white gloves. After I took them off, I felt lost. I had no relationship with the Lord. One Sunday morning, I thought usher board number one was serving. I dressed in my white uniform. When I arrived, usher board number two members were dressed in black. I was lost and embarrassed. Unfortunately, I could not continue my membership with that church. That was my last day at that church.

My new house wasn't a home. The house was beautiful, built from the ground up. I was excited but I had no clue how to make it a home. I worked two full-time jobs and couldn't enjoy it. I had a horrible relationship with my teenage daughter. She didn't feel loved, and I didn't show her love. My beautiful daughter had no clue that her mother was a train wreck. She didn't know why I was strict and hard. She had her own bedroom and bathroom. As a matter of fact, she had two bedrooms, plenty of clothes, a computer, and a bike. She had almost everything. The one thing she didn't have and needed the most was a loving mother. When I looked at her, I didn't want another person like me in the earth. I didn't want her to have sex before marriage and be a teen mom. I didn't want her to have bad credit, struggle, be beaten and abused, or have so many sex partners that she could lose count. I just didn't want her to be me!

In my strength, the only way I knew how to not make her like me was to reject her. I preferred she die before being another me. I was a walking time bomb, full of anxiety, depression, and grief and suicidal at the same time. No one knew the severity of my depression. By keeping up my outer appearance, I hid it from everyone. Whenever I entered a place, I made a fashion statement. It was a cover up. I started taking medication for everything...to sleep, smile, and live. I was fighting for my life. I was afraid my daughter was going to relive everything I was enduring.

I kept pulling of the scabs from losing my dad, the thoughts and trauma from abuse, and reliving the abortions I had. I was using medication, but it did not heal my broken heart. I opened up to people outside of my family. Sadly, they used my hurt against me and spread my pain like the tabloids.

Everyone outside my family that I divulged my torture to told others at work and spread my pain like the tabloids. I isolated from everyone except my daughter and husband. I tried my best to keep up an image that I had a perfect life. Every night, I fought not to commit suicide. My daughter and husband had no clue.

The year of 1999 was a rollercoaster ride with many hills and big drops. I was 30 years old. One day in the spring, I was invited to Spirit of Faith Christian Center. I thank God for the invite.

It was the covering needed in my life. During my first visit, the assistant pastor was singing a beautiful welcoming song. I was the only visitor that day and the solo was directly meant for me.

The soloist looked me in my eye and said, "You won't leave here like you came in. Jesus' name!"

I was overwhelmed by the love, greeting, and joy from everyone. I cried so hard that my tears could not stop flowing. What truly sealed the deal for me was the end of the service when the pastor gave the altar call for salvation, the infilling of the Holy Spirit, and to join the church. I received salvation and re-dedicated my life to Jesus my Lord and Savior. The pastor shared that he asked God to send all the world's rejects to his ministry. He wanted the drunks, crackheads, drug dealers, prostitutes, and everyone that society had given up on. I was neither of those individuals, but I was a reject. I was depressed, abused, grief ridden, angry, broken, and crazy, and on the edge of trying to commit suicide. I believed the pastor was a man after God's heart and God placed me there on purpose. When you know God has planted you in a ministry, you don't have a right to move away on your own. I realized that my life and house would not be the same.

Chapter 4

THE UNCOVERING BEGAN

In the beginning of my new life with Christ, I uncontrollably sobbed for God to help me become who He wanted me to be. I gave up my rights in my heart, but my mind had a long way to go. I didn't know where to look in the Bible for anything, and so, I started from the beginning. At the time, I didn't know Holy Spirit had already began speaking to me. Everything I heard from my heart was loving and good. The first instruction from the Lord was to stop drinking alcohol and being drunkard. Immediately, I surrendered and stop getting drunk. It wasn't an issue. I searched for the Scripture and came across Ephesians 5:18, it states, "And be not drunk with wine, wherein is excess; but be filled with the Spirit." The second instruction was for me to not do my pastors any harm by words or actions. I was not to allow people in my presence to talk evil over them. I didn't understand why the Holy Spirit had to instruct me not to do that concerning my pastors. I loved them, and that wouldn't have crossed my mind. A time came when I had to end a friendship due to that person speaking ill of my pastors. Chronicles 16:22 declares, "Saying, Touch not mine anointed, and do my prophets no harm." The Holy Spirit told me I was God's anointed too.

I began to pray and spend a lot of time on my knees while sobbing and crying out to God for help. I prayed for my pastors, daughter, family, mom, husband, his children, my daddy, my friend Kim, and everything that wasn't nailed down. For the first year, I found myself back at the alter repenting, receiving Holy Spirit about 20 times, and rededicating my life back to Christ. Sundays and Wednesdays in church was the only time I felt safe and confident. Every other day, I was fighting, cursing, having suicidal thoughts, and clubbing, but didn't drink any liquor. All this was happening while knowing I was where God wanted me to be in my church home.

Had I ever left the church? Yes, absolutely. I was miserable and my life quickly fell apart. I returned. I wasn't gone so long that I was missed. I repented and jumped back in the Lord's open arms. One thing about my church home was that I was taught the Word of God, but it was my duty to make every man a liar and study to know the Scriptures for myself. I received help learning how to connect with God. The only way was to spend time with Him. The more I spent time with God, the more I was able

23

to receive his love for me. Just like with my daddy, I spent a great deal of time getting to know his love for me, I had to do the same with Father God.

Transitioning from the First Sunday to the Lord's Table

"Wherefore whosoever shall eat this bread, and drink this cup of the Lord, unworthily, shall be guilty of the body and blood of the Lord!" reads 1 Corinthians 11:27. The first Sunday of every month used to be an evening with the male strippers at the club. I looked forward going to the club to eat the wings with mambo sauce. I went dressed to impress with less than $20 in my pocket. The strippers might have wondered why I didn't give them any money. It was them or the chicken wings and a drink. I chose the wings and drink every time.

Once I came to the first Sunday around the Lord's Table, I didn't look to go to the club again. The first thing the pastor ministering Holy Communion asked everyone to do was to examine ourselves to see if there was any unforgiveness, hatred, backbiting, or anything else that would prevent us from participating to release it. I didn't take communion that day. I was full of unforgiveness and anger toward others and overwhelmed with grief. Once again, I sobbed while on my knees, praying to God to help me release all my hurt and pain towards everyone. Little by little and a willing heart to live for God, I was becoming the woman who was already in me. I was ready to eat at the Lord's Table. Eating at the Lord's Table had become a part of my everyday regiment, not just on the first Sunday of every month. Taking communion is anytime I think about the goodness of the price paid for my life through Jesus. I take communion on behalf of others. Whenever there is sickness, disease, or any attack on my body, I take communion until that attack is destroyed.

Costly Cover Up

Philippians 2:3-4 (NIV) states, "Do nothing out of selfish ambition or vain conceit. Rather, in humility value others above yourselves, not looking to your own interests but each of you to the interests of the others." The cover up financially cost me. My cover-ups were the biggest deception in my mind. My outer appearance was the biggest band-aid. It's amazing how since I'm delivered, it's easy for me to identify another sister in Christ or woman who is dealing with this same stronghold I had. Covering pain and depression with material things only masked the symptoms. Because of my stronghold, it was hard to receive a compliment. When someone gave me a compliment, I automatically second-guessed their admiring words. I took that compliment and ran it through my tortured mind, which did more damaged. My tortured mind had me believing that people were jealous of me, talking about me, or wanted to be me. My insecure tormented mind had me believing the opposite as well. "You look terrible. You are too fat. Others look better that you," I heard. I constantly competed with myself. I was never enough.

Everything had to be picture-perfect. No matter what the event or function I was attending, I had to make a statement. The event was a simple cookout. I spent more than five-hundred dollars and I wasn't required to bring anything. I paid over six-hundred dollars for an outfit to attend a baby shower. The gift for the baby was up to fifty dollars. Just a day with friends meeting up to chat cost me three-hundred dollars. Special events at church cost me more than three-hundred dollars and the offering I gave was no more than $20.00 for each session. Because of my stronghold, I ended up spending money I really didn't have. Before attending any event, I checked many items: $100-$300 for hair, $135 for nails and feet, $55 for eyelashes, $100 for shoes, $200 or more for outfits, $37 for a carwash, $100 for fashion jewelry including earrings, necklace, and bracelets. At times I purchased a brand-new purse for $600 or more.

I was backed up in my bills and caused many unnecessary strains on my husband to get us out of the mess I got us into. My husband gave me the money to pay the bills, and I had my paychecks too. I shopped, shopped, and shopped, and most times, I gave the items away. I even shopped for others and didn't collect the money I paid for them. Because of overextending myself, I had to file bankruptcy several times to repay my debts.

To keep my addiction from my husband, I began to borrow money from others. I always repaid the money I borrowed, and so it became easier for me to borrow again from those who would lend me money. I knew how to dig myself out of it. I got two and three jobs to catch up. I was a hard worker, so my name was good in my field of work. People created a job for me when I needed one.

Anyone who knows me knew I had a thing for designer handbags. I would have an eight-hundred-dollar purse on my shoulder with less than five dollars to my name. Sometimes I didn't have lunch money, but I walked the streets at lunchtime with that designer purse on my shoulder and watched others eat. I was hungry, but pride would not allow me to ask for food from my co-workers. When I was asked how lunch was, I responded that it was great. Weak and hungry, I ate the leftovers from the meetings in our office. This cycle went on for years, all to cover my depression and tortures during my life. I had to learn how to trust God by putting him first over my finances. Things began to change once I became a cheerful giver into the kingdom of God. I love being a tither.

I can't leave this out. Oh my, I took my cover up to a new level of deception when using social media. To hide my pain, I became a professional photographer of myself. I took over ten pictures to get that one angle I felt was right! While at events taking pictures with others, if I felt like I didn't look right in that photo, I didn't post it. When I thought I looked right, no matter how everyone else looked, I posted that picture. My smile looked more like a frown in all my pictures. Yet, I received many likes or thumbs up. This is happening more and more in the body of Christ. The enemy, the devil, is getting deceptive with this particular stronghold. We as Christian must deal with it and come clean. We are losing too many mighty women and men in the body to this deception.

My prayer is that my testimony will help anyone who is dealing with a tortured mind to be free and seek help. Not everyone will use your pain against you. Start with inviting Jesus into your life, and as you receive His love,

He will help you. You are not alone. None of us are perfect, but we are perfect in Jesus!

Chapter 5

MY SPIRITUAL FATHER

When I was a little girl, I kept doing things and got into trouble. One summer day, my mom spanked me for something I did and told me I couldn't go outside to play the rest of the week. I woke up early in the morning just to look out the window. Since I was on punishment, I knew I wouldn't be going outside to play. I saw the neighborhood mechanic. He always wore a jumpsuit, his hands were dirty and oily, and he wore a pair of dress shoes. For the life of me, I couldn't understand why he wore dress shoes. As usual, the mechanic was under the car. It seemed like he had been working on the same car for the past 10 years. The car was elevated on jacks and the radio was playing. At the time, the radio was the only part of the car that worked. Occasionally, the mechanic attempted to start the engine. Some of the men from the neighborhood sometimes hung out around the car and tried to help the mechanic, but they did more talking than helping. Mind you, everyone in our neighborhood assumed he was a real mechanic and knew what he was doing. I watched as neighbor walked over to the mechanic and told him he was having a problem with his car and asked if he could fix it. The mechanic nodded. I assumed he agreed to fix the neighbor's car.

I later learned that the radio was a boom box positioned in the trunk of the car and was attached to the extension cord coming from lower-level apartment window.

The word got out among our neighbors not to let him touch their cars because he ruined the neighbor's car. The neighbor needed brakes and tire change. The mechanic ripped out the back seat, didn't fix the brakes or change the tire. Why didn't anyone notice that the mechanic was wearing the wrong shoes!

Unfortunately, we live in a time where many pastors wear the wrong shoes. Like the neighborhood mechanic, they appear to know something that they don't. They are false prophets and in the role of a pastor for the wrong reasons. They sleep with the women in the church, party, curse, drink, and misuse the money given to the church by the members. These false teachers mislead faithful believers and harbor debt and family confusion within their own homes.

However, I am blessed that my pastor, Apostle Mike Freeman, has truly been a blessing to me, my family, and the body of Christ. He taught me how to believe God for my life and family. My pastor shares the Word of God with laughter and love, so much so that anyone who wants to change can be changed with a renewed mind. My pastor makes forgiveness look easy. For more than twenty-one years, I've watched countless people betray him, talk about him, and leave him after many years of sowing into their lives. Apostle Mike kept forgiveness at the forefront. He has blessed and loved on the children in the church, the community, and wherever God had him to.

I went to church on Memorial Day weekend in the year of 2000. I packed my car before going to church because I was going to drive to see my daddy's grave and hang out for a couple of days after service. That morning, Pastor Mike jokingly, but seriously, shared the Word of God concerning death and the grave.

He said, "Some of y'all after service are ready to just hang out at the cemetery all day. You have your lawn chairs, grills, blankets, picnic baskets, and you are going to have an old good time."

I laughed so hard that tears came out my eyes. He was talking about me. I couldn't stop laughing. He shared Luke 24:6 (KJV) which read, "Why seek ye the living among the dead? He is not here, but is risen: remember how he spoke unto you when he was yet in Galilee." Another Scripture Pastor Mike shared was 2 Corinthians

5:8 KJV: "We are confident, I say and willing rather to be absent from the body and to be present with the Lord." On that day, I was set free from the grief of the grave. I kept a picture book with six different angles of my dad lying in his casket. I also had the negatives just in case I lost my pictures. After leaving church that day, I didn't go to my daddy's grave. I went home and grabbed those pictures and the negatives and cut them into pieces. I was free! I released my brothers and sisters from the anger I harbored because they didn't visit my dad's grave. I didn't go back to visit our dad's grave.

I sometimes cry when I think about my daddy, but it's not like before. I no longer cry and make myself so sick that I end up in the emergency room. We are reminded on Easter to *remember* our Lord and Savior Jesus' death, burial, and resurrection. I believe this is how we can remember our loved ones who have gone onto glory. God gave us a wonderful memory, a camera, and now video. We can focus on the good times. I had 25 wonderful years with my dad on earth. I no longer lose control on April 15th. I continuously pray for those who have lost loved ones by someone taking their lives in an act of evil. In many cases, the families are left with unanswered questions. I pray for all who are grieving, and I share my story whenever I can.

Another time when my pastor gave me a word from God was during a pivotal time in my life. I was on the verge of getting in trouble for disciplining my daughter. Most of the time, my daughter didn't deserve the spankings I gave her. She had no clue that I was distressed, depressed, and battling my own demons while fighting for my life. She often acted out and behaved badly. I simply lost it and went off. The situation had become extremely volatile, and it was no longer safe for either of us. In October of 2004, my daughter decided to move to Florida with people she met on online. I was devastated! All sorts of things began running through my mind. She was underage, and I didn't know anything about the people she decided to live with. Desperately seeking help, I called the church that day about 20 times. When I didn't like what the pastoral staff told me, I hung up and called the next pastoral staff member. By the time I got to Pastor Mike, I was tired. He spoke to me, and I was shocked by his words. At that moment, I was mentally and emotionally exhausted and couldn't receive what he was saying to me. It was simply unthinkable. I gathered myself as best I could and slowly began to process what my pastor was saying to me. Suddenly I could feel the ton of mental weight I had been carrying start lifting off me.

Pastor said, "Let her go!" He continued, "You are about to lose everything. This girl is running you ragged."

Now that was boldness in the Lord! It was painful to hear but needed to be said. I did what my pastor, a true man of God, instructed. I released my daughter and let her go. Pastor referred me to the Word of God in the book of Luke, Chapter 15: 11-24 (KJV):

"And he said, A certain man had two sons: And the younger of them said to his father, Father, give me the portion of goods that falleth to me. And he divided unto them his living. And not many days after the younger son gathered all together, and took his journey into a far country, and there wasted his substance with riotous living. And when he had spent all, there arose a mighty famine in that land; and he began to be in want. And he went and joined himself to a citizen of that country; and he sent him into his fields to feed swine. And he would fain have filled his belly with the husks that the swine did eat: and no man gave unto him. And when he came to himself, he said, How many hired servants of my father's have bread enough and to spare, and I perish with hunger! I will arise and go to my father, and will say unto him, Father, I have sinned against heaven, and before thee, and am no more worthy to be called thy son: make me as one of thy hired scrvants. And he arose, and came to his father. But when he was yet a great way off, his father saw him, and had compassion, and ran, and fell on his neck, and kissed him. And the son said unto him, Father, I have sinned against heaven, and in thy sight, and am no more worthy to be called thy son. But the father said to his servants, Bring forth the best robe, and put it on him; and put a ring on his hand, and shoes on his feet: And bring hither the fatted calf, and kill it; and let us eat, and be merry: For this my son was dead, and is alive again; he was lost, and is found. And they began to be merry."

He also instructed me to keep praying for my daughter and to be ready to receive her when she returned. Due to their lack of understanding, my family was upset and angry when I shared the pastor's words and told them that I was going to do as he instructed me. I released my daughter and went on with my life. I prayed for and thought about my baby every day, but I didn't inquire about her whereabouts. I stood on God's Word that she would be okay and return.

I accepted a new job in January in another city. Things were moving fast, and I quickly began adjusting to the new chapter in my life. Although I had no contact with her, I still of thought of my daughter and to prayed for her daily. My daughter remained in touch with my mom; the two of them have always been close. I hadn't heard anything for at least four or five months. I continued to pray for her but didn't ask about her. One morning, around two o'clock, I received a call from my mother. Immediately I thought something was wrong or someone died. She told me that my daughter was on the phone.

My baby, with a cracking and tearful voice asked, "Can I come home?"

I immediately responded, "Absolutely! As a matter of fact, come to me and we will go home together on the weekend."

That was one of the best days of my life. My baby was coming back home, just like Pastor said she would.

My Pastor advised me many times, and I haven't always immediately obeyed him, especially when it came to my husband. I confided in Pastor about the infidelity in my marriage. I was aware of it and willingly accepted. Pastor Mike doesn't play around with words. He gives it to you honest and straight.

Pastor Mike said, "Get out of it. This man does not love you!"

At the time, my husband wasn't living a Christian life or attending church with me. My Pastor was more concerned about me. He often ministered to the women in the church about settling for less than God's best. I did my best to explain that we loved each other and had many years together. Pastor didn't waver in his response to me. He repeated what he said.

He often told the women in church, "Don't be a dumb woman!"

It seemed harsh, but some of us needed to hear it.

As hard as it was, believe it or not, it was easier when Pastor told me to let my daughter go. To let my husband go went over my head and I couldn't wrap my brain around that! At the time, even though I knew God was speaking through my Pastor, I couldn't and wouldn't receive those words. I wasn't ready or willing to release my husband. As I began to truly think about it and trust God, I saw things for what it was. Change had to come, and change did come. For a lot of the believers in the body of Christ, we can't seem to wrap our minds around letting our children go, but we will be quick to let go of our spouses.

Every time I needed my pastor, he was there for me. All I had to do was to study the Word of God and get familiar with the Father's voice. It was important for me get a copy of every lesson that was relevant to me so that I could go over it whenever I wanted it. I received countless impartations about my life from my pastor. The most important was how to love and forgive others. Pastor taught me how to use my faith when the odds seemed against me. He has consistently shown me and my family unconditional love. My Spiritual Dad did not replace my daddy. His presence continued to move me closer to my Heavenly Father's unconditional love and acceptance through Jesus! Thank you, Apostle Mike!

Chapter 6
MY FIRST LADY

"She openeth her mouth with wisdom; and in her
tongue is the law of kindness!"

- Proverbs 31:26

I't's not often when someone finds a beautiful woman
with a beautiful heart. She either has one or the other,
and to have both is priceless! My first lady has both outer
beauty and inner beauty. The love she has for women is
indescribable. Her heart's desire is for every woman to
know that she is valued, and that Jesus paid the price for
her value. Titus 6:3-5 (KJV) states, "The aged women
likewise, that they be in behaviour as becometh holiness,
not false accusers, not given to much wine, teachers of
good things; That they may teach the young women to be
sober, to love their husbands, to love their children, To be
discreet, chaste, keepers at home, good, obedient to their
own husbands, that the word of God be not blasphemed."
My first lady truly gave me sound guidance when I needed
it the most. As a babe in Christ, I didn't know how to pray
or believe in God for anything. I was consumed with
trying to be perfect on the outside, but my heart and mind

was oppressed. In the year of 2000, I scheduled an appointment to meet with her concerning budgeting. The meeting went well.

When our meeting was about to close, she asked me, "Are you married?"

Quietly, like a baby, I said, "Yes."

It was the beginning of a life-changing experience.

"Are you happy?"

I simply replied, "Yes, but it's complicated."

"Sit back down."

I began to share my story. It seemed unbelievable to her, but she didn't judge me.

She responded, "If you feel you can handle it and can take it, then stand by your man." She continued, "Sherrie, but by the Spirit of the Lord, if you give it up, you can have it all!"

Pastor said the same thing, but boldly different. It took me ten years to finally get it. First Lady then asked if I was filled with the Holy Spirit with evidence of speaking in other tongues.

"Dr. Dee, I've been up at the altar about 20 times to receive Holy Spirit and I don't have it!"

"I was wondering why you keep coming to the front every Sunday. Don't come up there no more...it's in you."

Now, when your pastor tells you not to come to the front no more, you've been up there too many times!

In the same meeting I was asked about my children. I have three: two sons and one daughter combined with my husband. I shared with Dr. Dee some of the challenges I was having with my daughter.

"When you leave my office, go and purchase the book *Prayers that Avail Much* from our bookstore. There is a prayer in it for a teenager. Pray that prayer over your daughter daily," she advised.

My life was changed. I learned how to pray using the Scriptures according to God's Word. I took full advantage of any help I could get. I discovered how to better pray for others and worship God as well.

I had a trying time with my daughter on my wedding anniversary on January 17, 2002. It was a Wednesday, and I had the day off from work. I planned to have a day at the salon. My daughter was in school. Before leaving, I turned her room upside down. I wanted her to clean it up like I said. I took the cords from her computer so that she couldn't use it until she cleaned her room. When she returned home, I hadn't returned to correct her about her room. Well, she flipped out and busted a window in the house! She was smart. Afterward, she called the church and spoke with a minister in the youth department. I was still in the hair salon when I received the call from the minister. She asked me to come to see her after my hair was finished.

I said, "I'll be up now."

My stylist was on her break, and so my hair was half complete. When I spoke with the minister and found out what my daughter had done, I was hot! I was steaming with anger.

I stormed back to the hair salon, grabbed my purse, and deep-down sighed, "Jesus, I'm going to kill this girl!"

As I proceeded to the parking lot, my pastor and first lady pulled up. I waved and rushed pass them with a messy wet nose and tears streaming down my face. Dr. Dee came to me from afar. All I saw was her big, beautiful eyes filled with tears. She knew I was done! All I had was murder on my mind. I was so hurt.

"Sherrie, come here please. Do it for me."

When others show they really care, it means the world when you are hurting. I saw the care in her eyes. I explained what happened. She loved on me and took the time to help. She returned to the hair salon with me and asked the stylist to finish my hair. The stylists started praying in the spirit for me. They knew I've had several set-off moments. I entered the hair salon on our church grounds upset many times. The stylists prayed in the spirit for me without saying a word to me. The overwhelming love from those ladies helped me to make it through.

I stayed at church all day until Bible study started. My daughter came to church with my husband. When I saw her, fire seemed to burn in my mind. I thank God for my pastors. That night, they took my daughter home with them, which gave me time to calm down. I was headed straight to the jail if I would have laid one finger on my daughter. The devil had a plan, but God had a purpose!

Another time Dr. Dee reached out to me by phone while I was at work. She called my job because my daughter needed someone to talk to me about making her sign up for a girl's organization. It didn't dawn on me at the time what I was making her do. I always wanted to join the girls' group when I was young, but it didn't happen. I truly wanted my daughter to experience and be everything I didn't get a chance to do while growing up.

Dr. Dee, with a loving and caring voice, said to me, "Now Sherrie, she doesn't want to join the girl's group. Your daughter is fifteen years old."

I explained how rebellious she was becoming and how I felt that the other ministers had begun to disrespect my authority. I mentioned how some of them took my daughter home without my permission. They just told me that they were taking her home with them. At the time, she wasn't listening to me. I accepted any help I could get. Dr. Dee addressed those issues, and I was wasn't disrespected again by those individuals. Yes, I was a saved *ghetto* mom, but I belonged to God, just like everyone else. Dr. Dee has always shown me love, acceptance, and kindness.

One time at one of our women's conferences, I wore a bright colored jacket that I loved. It was a cute sequin jacket with the numbers of my birth month on the front that I purchased online. I wore it well. I was taking pictures and felt so good with that jacket on. I didn't know that the color combination was a representation of a sorority. Throughout the day, I learned all about the sorority. I met some friendly sorority members that shared the history and other more demanding sorority members. I was pointed out throughout the day about not being a member of that sorority. I was a little annoyed and was trying to keep smiling and serving because I was also a part of GGG ministry working at the event. Dr. Dee came past, and I shared what was happening.

Dr. Dee looked me in my eyes and said, "Wear what you want and be okay with it. I mean it. Wear what you want."

The devil was trying to attack my mind with the shame of embarrassment. At that moment, I just wanted to return to my hotel room for the night and miss out on what God had for me. I was angry. If one more person said something to me about wearing the jacket, I was going to curse them out at the conference. God is always in the mist of when you need Him the most. One more person did say something to me. She asked where I purchased the jacket. I looked online to see if the seller had more, but it was sold out. I blessed her with my jacket and gave it to her the next day. She was happy and grateful. I thanked God for Dr. Dee's input. My fear of rejection of what others thought and said to me was about to have me run into a shell.

Dr. Dee Dee is the only woman who told me to shut up and I wasn't offended. I felt loved when those words came out of her mouth. Twenty-one years later, I still hear it when I'm about to say something I can't take back. As it relates to responding to my husband, I hear her voice loud and clear, "Shut up!"

When I joined Spirit of Faith, I kept two things in my make-up bag. I had a black eyeliner for my brows, eyes, and lips along with a tube of clear lip gloss. One day, Dr. Dee shared at one of our WWW meetings how to apply make-up.

She said, "Stop lining your lips up with that black pencil."

In so many words, it was ugly. She began to share with the women how to apply makeup. She gave away some brand-new products. She loved to bless others. At the same meeting, she had some of the stylists from our hair salon share how to use a flat iron properly. It was informational and helpful. A lot of us were frying our hair like chicken. What a blessing. She shared with us how we could tell if our clothing may be a hindrance.

"If your outfit forms into a question mark in the back, then it's too tight."

I thought that if it wasn't tight, it wasn't right. She began to share that we represented God and we should not be a hindrance to our brothers or another sister's husband. I discarded my cat suits and see-through clothing.

Dr. Dee hosted an unrecorded married women's meeting with the wives in the church. The information shared with us from our woman of God was life changing! Dr. Dee was honest, loving, and at the same time, serious when it came to keeping it together while it seemed like everything was falling apart. One advice she gave to us was that we should not talk about our husbands to anyone.

"Never allow people to talk about your husband...not your family, his family, your girlfriends, his friends, and most definitely never at the workplace. You can't pray and speak negative at the same time," she explained.

During that meeting she also spoke to us about keeping up ourselves.

"Just because you had a baby or babies don't mean you should stop taking care of yourselves. The same way you kept yourself in the beginning, you are going to have continue."

One sister-in-Christ stood up to ask a question about what she should do since her husband no longer paid her any attention. He was more into the video games.

"You let yourself go. Give him something to look forward to."

Dr. Dee asked her when the last time her hair had been done. Although it may have sounded like a putdown, it wasn't. Dr. Dee blessed her with a hairdo by one of the stylists in our hair salon. Now mind you, I had things going in my marriage that wasn't going great, but I was there to receive whatever God had for me through my woman of God. Dr. Dee touched on the marriage bed. She talked about being fulfilled in the marriage bed and shared with us about the *big O*! I was lost. I had no clue as to what she was talking about. She gave us instructions how to trigger it and go for the *big O*!

Before my husband, I had a lot of weeds in my garden. I thank God for His promise that all things become new and old things have passed away! My *weed* was the men I slept with before my husband. In the beginning of our relationship, my husband was a weed too. I needed a weedkiller...Jesus.

Dr. Dee commanded us not to use our bodies as a weapon against our husband by holding back. She stated that after a while, your husband may not want it! After the meeting I went home, showered, and put what I learned earlier into practice concerning the *big O*. The awesomeness of God concerning that area is that God saved it for my husband! I felt like a virgin. It was my first time. Dr. Dee must have forgot to mention the *big O* was going to knock me out for the rest of the night. I ran into one of my ex-weeds and he tried to remind me of the good times we had. Not trying to hurt his feelings, but baby we didn't have anything! I used Scripture to let him know that I was a new creature in Christ and old things had passed away! God is good!

I'm often asked by people if I had spent personal time with Dr. Dee. They wanted to know if I had been to her home, to dinner, or just hanging out with her. I normally responded that I hung out with her all the time...on my lunch break, in my family room, driving in my car, and whenever I need a reminder. I'm a behind the scenes person. I love whatever time I'm given. I have every DVD or CD of the service. When I want to spend time with my 1st Lady, I can.

Dr. Dee continues to pour out her heart to woman around the world. She is a bridge to help woman to know that no matter what our past looked like, God loves us and will use our story for His glory. Thank you, Dr. Dee, for your endless love and prayers towards me and other women. I love how you encourage women to believe God for everything. I love how you helped me to birth the gifts within me and believe God for anything. I truly understand that the work that needs to be done in the earth will be done through God's people. You are an amazing woman. May God continue to bless you and let your light shine! I love you dearly!

Chapter 7

YES, BY HIS STRIPES I'M HEALED

But he was wounded for our transgressions, he was
bruised for our iniquities: the chastisement of our peace
was upon him; and with his stripes we are healed.

- Isaiah 53:5

On Sunday, May 3, 2015 during our Holy Communion service, my husband and I got into a small argument. He felt like I was stealing communion. I did take two extra prefilled communion cups and placed them in my purse. I heard God say to take two cups. I walked around with those communion cups in my purse for about four weeks. I didn't feel bad about having them, but I was unsure why God had me take them. "By His Stripes I'm Healed!" is what I heard the most in my new life with Christ! I spoke it, but in my heart and mind, I didn't receive it until I had to rely on it. I was in trouble.

Back in 2013, I went to the emergency room several times. I felt ill but didn't know the reason. I did have issues with high blood pressure, but for the most part, I was healthy. Every test result was normal except my white blood count. The doctor explained that it was extremely high, which meant that I was fighting off some type of infection. For the following two years, I was in and out of the emergency room. Finally, my primary care doctor referred me to the Cancer and Blood Center in June of 2015. He couldn't determine why my white blood count kept elevating. Upon arriving for my first appointment on June 1, 2015, I walked to the directory panel to find the Cancer and Blood Center. I went to the door. I didn't like the sign on the door. Cancer. I was mad! The doctors drew a huge amount of blood to be tested. The doctor explained that the process takes months to find out the type of problem I had. I didn't believe it would take that long. I asked about the next steps. I needed a bone marrow test. I didn't want to drag it out, and so I asked about the next opening for the test. I was scheduled for a bone marrow test on June 5, 2015. The test was extremely painful. Afterward, I was wheeled out to my husband. I was in so much pain. A piece of my bone was extracted from my right backside. As we were leaving the center, my husband, who is an excellent driver, backed into a pole and damaged our car. I knew it was a spirit of fear that overtook him. He wasn't happy about how I looked at that moment. I wasn't the wife of faith. I was discouraged and fearful. On June 8, 2015, I was schedule for an MRI and

CAT scan. On June 11, 2015, I was given the results, and I was pissed! I wish I could have punched the devil in his face! I was told that I had three masses in my body. The lymph nodes in my throat area were enlarged. I had two masses in my colon. The one near my rectal area was the size of a lemon. A mass on my right breast was also found. The doctor explained that they will have to do a biopsy of the one near my rectal area. That was the one they could reach. The test was schedule for Monday, June 15, 2015.

The day before my biopsy, I attended church. Praise and worship was odd. We couldn't move on with service because the praise and worship ministry flowed most of the service. Our assistant pastor interrupted the service and said that the praise was for an evil report that someone received. He said to get down there so we could agree that whatever the report, it was sent back to the pits of hell from where it came. I went down to agree with him, and he laid hands on me along with others. I had on my sunshades. I was crying but more than anything, I was angry about the report from the doctor. I felt sucker-punched by the devil. When I left church, I truly felt in my heart that every mass in my body was destroyed.

Monday, June 15th at 7:00 am I was to have the biopsy. My husband asked if I wanted him to stay with me while the procedure was done. I didn't want him to wait. Once in the doctor's office, they explained that another sonogram had to be done to see where to stick the needle for the tissue from my rectal area. I had no problem with it. While sitting in the waiting area, God told me to take out one of the communion cups and take it, but also remind Him why I take communion.

I said, "God, I take this communion because number one, it is in remembrance of your son Jesus and the price he paid for me and number two, I do this because you commanded me to, and by his stripes I'm healed."

I went to the room to have the sonogram. I laid on the table and fell into a deep sleep. When I woke up, five people stood around and looked at me.

The head doctor stated, "Mrs. Walker, we can't do the biopsy. We don't see the two masses in your colon."

One doctor drove from Fairfax, Virginia to Waldorf, Maryland to collect the tissue. He was angry for the wasted time. The mass they were looking to take the tissue from was the size of a lemon near my rectum. That was two down and one more mass to be destroyed.

On Thursday, June 18th, I was scheduled for mammogram on my right breast. Again, while waiting in the waiting room God told me to take out the other communion cup and take it and remind Him why I take communion.

I said, "God, I take this communion because number one, it is in remembrance of your son Jesus and the price he paid for me and number two, I do this because you commanded me to, and by his stripes I'm healed," I replied.

The mammogram was complete, and the doctor came in to tell me what he saw.

"Mrs. Walker, this mass is the same mass we put a marker on two years ago. The mass has shrunk in size since the last time we saw you. You are free to go," he explained.

I returned to my primary doctor. He was astonished by the latest findings. I was retested, and my white blood count went down and the lymph nodes in my neck were no longer enlarged.

Two years later, while working as a temporary employee moving towards becoming permanent, I woke up around 5:00 in the morning with the worst headache I ever had. I wondered if my husband hit me by mistake in my sleep. Absolutely not, he would not do that to me. My head was still pounding as I headed out to go to work. I didn't want the television on while I dressed and didn't turn on the music in the car. I was in bad shape. Normally, I prayed and read the *Daily Word* to my husband while going into work. I just wanted silence. My day at work didn't start until 10:00 am. From seven until I was to start work, I was at my desk with my head down. My supervisor was ready to begin the overview of the previous day. I was in her office, and she noticed that my speech was off, and words were slurred.

"Sherrie, you don't look good. You are having a stroke."

She wanted to call 911.

I asked, "Please don't. I don't want to make a scene."

Our office was five blocks away from the hospital. I told her I would catch a cab. She gave me $5.00. I walked outside to catch a cab. The meter on the cab was at $4.95 and I needed to go one more block. I told the driver I only had $5.00 and if he could still take me to the emergency room.

"No," he responded.

I had to walk a block and a half to the emergency room. Once I arrived, the admission personal immediately called a code over the loudspeaker. I was rushed to the back, my clothes were stripped off, and I was rushed in for a CAT scan.

"Give her the clot buster now! Now!" someone yelled.

God was with me. I had a brain hemorrhage, not a stroke. The attack was formed but it didn't prosper. The doctor explained to me that I shouldn't have made it. Too many hours from the time I woke up to getting to the hospital had passed. I left the hospital the next day without any side effects from the hemorrhage. God had my 72 thousand angels encamped around me. I trusted God for complete healing. Taking communion is my lifestyle. It is my first meal, and to this day, I still do it.

On March 18, 2021, my brother Carroll was in a horrible car accident. I received the call around 5:45 in the morning from my sister-in-love Cheryl. She could barely tell me what happened. All I heard was that my brother had to be cut out of the truck. I began to pray in my heavenly language, in the spirit. My brother is over 400 pounds and has some health issues. He survived the crash but has several broken bones. According to his medical team, his recovery will be a long journey. I know the true healer and his name is Jesus. The same God who healed me is the same God who has already brought my brother through, no matter what it looks like. I will and continue to take communion on my brother's behalf. God took me to the end of the attack on my brother's life. He will live and not die! My brother will come out without the smell of smoke. He will walk again, he will lose the weight, his health will be renewed, he will see his daughter graduate from high school, he will meet his son-in-law and grandkids in the future, and he will enjoy his latter years with his wife and family. I believe and receive it in the name of Jesus! I wrote this confession on Monday, March 30, 2021.

Always speak life over yourself and others. Don't allow anyone to pull you in a panic. Pull them into your peace! God has given us the ability to calm the storms of life. Remember, we always win! Celebrate the victory in advance.

THE PRODIGAL DAUGHTER

"I say to you that likewise there will be more joy in heaven over one sinner who repents than over ninety-nine just persons who need no repentance."

- Luke 15: 7 (NKJV)

Chapter 8

FROM ABUSER TO BROTHER IN CHRIST

"To subvert a man in his cause, the Lord approveth not."

- Lamentations 3:36

I had to look up in the dictionary what it is to subvert. It means to cause downfall, ruin, or destruction of. In this chapter, I wrote my experience with domestic violence. I want to help those that may be dealing with domestic violence and those that no longer are in this situation but haven't forgiven their abuser. While I am being used by God, I can't pick and choose what I want to share. During that chapter of my life, my mind shifted to low self-esteem, and I lost my self-worth. When I was in high school, my parents decided to separate. They divorced a year later. It was the beginning of losing my support system. My two older siblings stayed with my dad. My mother cared for the two youngest. My oldest sister was already living on her own. My mother was a hard-working woman. She worked two and sometimes three jobs to provide for our family. Without the strong supervision of my parents and older siblings, I got involved in too many things and people that were bad for me. I was 15 years old and went buck-wild. When I was supposed to be in the house after school, I was in the streets and having sex. I felt free to do whatever I wanted. I came back just in time before my mom was expected to be home.

Once I began dating a nice guy, I stopped partying. At first, it was beautiful. He brought me flowers, we went to the movies every week, and we wore matching shirts at times. He helped me get away from a guy in the neighborhood who was physically abusive to me. Not long after we started dating, he became abusive. I let him control my every being. He was a strong tower. I didn't give him any consequences. At first, he raised his voice. I showed fear in my eyes. Weeks later, he pushed me in my chest. Still, he had no consequences. Afterwards, nothing happened for a few days. I was numb and scared. I didn't tell anyone. It was one of my deepest and darkest secrets. He was not the person I or my family grew to love. I believed it wouldn't happen again. I was wrong. The beatings became intense. He struck my body, not my face. I still have skin damage on my left thigh, and I am ashamed to show my legs. I saw how he beat up men. He tortured those guys for not paying money they owed his friends. Some of the guys he beat up for no reason because of jealousy.

My abuser became the biggest force in my life. He isolated me from everyone who loved me by using verbal threats. My fear was overwhelming. Who my abuser was to me, he wasn't to others. He was a great guy to his friends, a loving family member, a great worker to his employer, and a great member to his church. So many will not believe who an abuser is to their victims. In many cases, abusers are found out when a victim dies. I thank God my story didn't end in my death. My abuser was a strong force. I forgot I had my daddy, brothers, 14 uncles, a host of male cousins, the police, my mom, and anyone else who loved me. In the beginning, my abuser didn't hit me in my face. The beatings were done to my body. He was a huge muscular guy, and back then, I weighed less than a hundred and twenty pounds. To end the relationship was not an option. I was so afraid that I endured the abuse for five years. I tried to date other guys, but they were too afraid of my abuser. He beat them up as well. Because of fear, I didn't let my family know about the beatings I endured on a daily basis. The mental abuse affected more than the physical. I knew when the punches were coming. I started to fight back. We both had scares, but I was no match for him.

He often said, "You ugly. You skinny. I don't know why I'm even dealing with you."

He even told me that he would be glad when I met someone else. The first time I was told I was ugly was by one of my father's brothers when I was eight years old; not knowing then I was learning how to hide abuse from my parents. It made me very sad. I didn't tell my dad or mom back then. To hear it again by my abuser brought that memory back to my mind. When I didn't get home from school at a certain time, he met at the bus stop to beat me. I started hooking school to be with him. Several times I tried to see other guys. Out of fear, I ended up back with him. One time when I was trying to get out of the relationship, I had a one-night stand. I visited the new guy on and off for about two months. My abuser became suspicious. The night he caught me, I was taken to a park and beaten. The worst thing he did, which took every ounce of self-esteem out of me, was to hulk-spit in my mouth and made me swallow it! He should have killed me. I was broken to my core—trauma. I thought I would not be kissed again. For years, I brushed my teeth several times a day. I felt dirty.

At the age of sixteen, I was pregnant with my daughter. The beatings became intense. I was punched in my stomach, had cuts on my feet, and I was dragged by him.

I didn't tell my family. My baby moved around and dogged every punch. I prayed often that my baby would live and not die. My beautiful baby girl was born with pink skin and a head full of straight black hair. She didn't look like me or my abuser. She looked like my one-night stand. I was confused, scared, and happy. My baby was healthy. Two weeks after giving birth, my abuser was told that my baby wasn't his. Months before my daughter was born, my family member was angry with me and informed others. I was hurt. I wondered why someone in my family would hurt me like that. I went serval years without speaking, and because I still loved that person, I eventually forgave.

I was ready to face my truth. I asked my abuser to get a blood test. He didn't want one because he believed that my baby was his because my daughter looked like his father. I told him not to ask for the test later because I wasn't going to give it to him. I'm so thankful that I wasn't a part of a tabloid talk show. I know I would have run to the back, fell over the couch, and left out the back door. He knew she wasn't his. I don't know why he refused to acknowledge it. The beatings got worse, yet he was loving to my baby girl. He truly liked light-skinned women with long curly hair. My baby resembled those ladies.

I was preparing to graduate from high school and looking forward to the prom. My abuser made it clear that he wasn't taking me, and he said that I wasn't going to my once-in-a-lifetime event. My prom was taken away from me. Everyone was excited, but they didn't understand why I wasn't going. I didn't make a big deal about it, but I wanted to go.

At seventeen, I was pregnant again. I continued to hide the abuse. He didn't want the baby and was forceful about getting rid of it. My parents didn't believe in abortion, and I couldn't tell them that I wasn't keeping the baby. I was five months into my pregnancy. The only way to abort the baby was to do a saline abortion. That was my second darkest pain. I felt it for years. My abuser was on the outside at the ground floor window of the hospital with his dog by his side. He wanted to make sure I went through with procedure. I was in a room with other teenage girls and women that knew it was the worst thing we could do to another human being. My baby's tiny little leg hung out of me for six hours. The nurses had a job to do, but they treated us like we were the worst patients they ever had. The labor was unbearable. I cried out for help. Afterwards, my baby was dropped in a pan to be discarded.

My shame and depression took a toll on me. My mom and dad weren't happy. I felt disconnected. My mom let me know that she didn't abort any of her children, no matter how bad things were. My parents still didn't know what was happening to me, only one of my closest friends. I tried to commit suicide by taking pills, but my oldest brother came over in time and called for help. I was transported to the hospital and had my stomach pumped. For a month, I was in the mental health wing in the same hospital where I had the abortion. The only person was allowed to see me was my mother. I wanted so bad to see my dad. My dad wasn't told about my condition at the time. He found out after the fact. I was too ashamed. I hid from my daddy. I thank God today that I don't have to hide or run anymore in life because of my Jesus. Praise break!

My abuser came to visit one evening. He said that I was stupid and walked out. I felt worthless. My mom came the next day to see me and brought my beautiful 11-month-old baby girl. She reached for me, but the doctors didn't allow me to hold her. I couldn't hold my baby. I was so hurt. Returning home to my mom to help me get through that hard time. My abuser started dating another young lady. Did I embrace my release out of that relationship? No. I was hurt and heartbroken. I begged and cried day in and day out over him. I wanted my dysfunctional abusive relationship back. Whenever my mom saw me, I was crying. One day, she called my abuser and asked him to come by so that she could talk to him. He came over. I was happy, but my mom didn't say what I thought she was going to say to him. My mom was firm.

She said, "There is going to come a time when Sherrie is not going to want you and there will be nothing you will be able to do to get her back."

"You're wrong mom. I will always love him. Why are you saying this?" I irrationally replied.

My mom was angry with me.

"I'm telling you what I know. You will not want to have anything to do with him."

That went completely over my head. He listened, laughed, and left.

Trying to move on was hard. I was allowed to move to Richmond, Virginia to live with my Uncle Jack and Aunt Bunny. They didn't have children, and so they welcome me and my daughter. I cried every single day. I could not function. My Uncle Jack didn't sugar-coat anything he said. He was wheelchair-bound.

One morning he wheeled over to me and explained, "Girl, you are not in love. You are too young to know what love is. You are in love with that hump and pump he is giving you. Once you meet someone else that can give it better, you will forget all about that boy!" He continued, "Now Aunt Bunny and I have love."

Uncle Jack was right!

I wondered why she stayed with Uncle Jack and married him. They were high school sweethearts. He went into the military and was injured while playing football. That happened before I was born. Aunt Bunny stayed by his side through all of it and they took care of each other. They stayed married until death, which was over 40 years.

I eventually moved back to Washington, D.C. To take care of my baby, I started working a full-time job. I bought myself some new clothes, got my hair done, and tried my best to move on. One evening after work, I was heading to the grocery store to purchase my baby's food for the week. I ran into my abuser. He began to accuse me of thinking that I was doing better without him. He followed me to the market while taunting, hitting, and pushing me. I was holding on to my baby's food and milk. As I was walking past an alley, he started to beat me up. I dropped my groceries and began to fight back, only to be beaten up more. My dress was ripped, and I was bleeding from my mouth. On top of that, he bit me on my shoulder bone. A friend of his came out of a house, not to help, but only to look and laugh. After so many blows to my head, I ran. I made it to my aunt's house a few blocks away and broke down in her driveway. My cousin came to help me. I woke up in the hospital. The doctor thought I was attacked by a dog because of the bite on my shoulder. They wanted to give me all sorts of shots for animal bites. My father knew something was awry. He was the only one who believed me when I told them that my abuser bit me. My family was in uproar. My friend could no longer keep her silence. She told my mother everything she knew. My family was ready to go to war. My mother filed a restraining order, and the court date was set.

Two days before the court date, I was home alone with my daughter. My abuser came over to apologize. He told me that he was sorry, he loved me, and would never hit me again.

"We are going to tell the judge we love each other, and we want our families to stay out of our relationship."

We had sex that day. I didn't tell anyone. The day of the hearing, he acted like he didn't know me. When it was time to hear our case, the judge said it had been dismissed. It was a set up...a hurtful setup. My mother asked why. The judge told her that I had been in contact with him. I tried to explain what happened. He told the judge he wanted an order for me to stay away from him. He didn't want me. He left the court laughing. I cried in despair, and my family consoled me.

A year passed. He returned with what I thought was a sincere apology to me and my family for everything he had done. Afterwards, all went well for a year and a few months. At that time, we were adults and living together. He started to beat me again. I began to urinate in my sleep. I could no longer hide the black eyes, scares, and bald spots in my hair. Due to my bruised face, my employer switched me to the third shift. They didn't want to fire me because I was a hard worker. To help me feel better, my friend and confidante did my hair. Within hours, he dumped water on my hair because I didn't get his permission. When I purchased new clothes without his permission, he threw them out the window. My self-esteem was gone. I couldn't understand how I allowed him to do those things to me. I blamed myself and felt like I deserved it. I also had to deal with verbal abuse from his family. Several were extremely hateful towards me. His parents were the nicest and they didn't show any hatred or disrespect towards me. I couldn't understand why he was so abusive. Still, I wasn't good enough to have his children. I was forced to have two more abortions.

One evening he beat me up without reason. He ripped my braids from my head and busted my lip. I told him that one day he was going get it back. It came a few hours later. He was shot three or four times that night. Still, I was afraid he would be dead by the time I saw him in the hospital. I prayed so hard for God to give him a second chance. When I entered the room after his surgery, the first thing he said to me was that he was so sorry for what he did.

"You said I would get it back one day," he stated.

I told him that I didn't mean it. I wanted him to just stay alive. I was told that while he was in the hospital, I should keep in mind that we weren't married, and my abuser had other friends. Those other friends happen to be other girlfriends. I was hurt and didn't go back to the hospital. A few weeks after returning to our apartment, he abused me again. I did everything to try to help him get back on his feet. I wiped his behind after every bowel movement, only to be hit in my head with his arm several times. He worn a cast. I was senseless and foolish. I knew it.

1990 The Year of Change!

One Saturday in late July, a large cookout was given for my abuser on his birthday. I wasn't welcomed or allowed to the event. I was banned from his parent's house due to fighting. I sat across the street at another neighbor's house so that he could keep an eye on me. He did offer me a plate of food, but I didn't eat. I was quite embarrassed. That day, I paged the beeper number I was given two weeks before. That moment was my physical exit. Mentally, I still had years to go. Nineteen days after his birthday was my birthday. My best friend and the gentleman took me out to eat to celebrate. It was a nice lunch, and I was given a piece of cake to take home with me. That evening, upon my abuser returning home from work, he was angry because I went out for lunch. He beat me up on my birthday, smashed the cake in my face, and busted my lip. After all of that he raped me. It wasn't consensual sex. While being raped, my tears rolled down my face. I smiled because I believed it was to be his last time hitting me, abusing me, and sleeping with me. I was done! In late August 1990, I broke ties with him for good. I met a gentleman who was much older than me. I was free, no longer connected to my abuser or anyone else who tormented me during that relationship.

My abuser was still loving and caring toward my daughter, even after finding out that he wasn't her father. He still told everyone my daughter was his. From time to time, he stopped by my mom's home to see my mother and daughter. I asked my mom to stop allowing him to come over. I was in a new relationship, and I wouldn't come over if she continued to let in my abuser. I felt like it was disrespectful to my new relationship. My mom eventually stopped the visits from him. In 1995, when my daddy passed away, he came to pay respect. That was the last time I saw him for a few years. He periodically called my job just to say hi and asked about my daughter. I eventually stop answering those calls.

Life for me was instantly better in my new relationship. I had new apartment, new car, and a better job. My outer appearance blossomed. I went from looking like a skinny fashion doll to a brick-house doll. I had an hourglass figure that was out of this world and my hair grew heathy and long. I did my best to run into my abuser so that he could see what he no longer had. I didn't see him. I saw others who could tell him about the new me. I was all in my flesh. I visited one of my mother's-in-Christ who lived on his street. She went up one side and came down the other side of me. She always called me Marie, never Sherrie. Mother J told me one day that she knew I was only coming over to see him.

She said, "Guess what? He just left."

We laughed, but she spoke the truth. She always had something good to eat so she fed me well. I loved me some Mother J.

I had the freedom that the world gives—fleshly freedom. That freedom was a cover up, but the brokenness was still there, just dormant for years. I thought I was free and delivered. After my father's death, hurtful experiences resurfaced in my mind.

Five years later in 2000 after surrendering my life to Christ, I began to ask God to help me overcome the thoughts of that painful experience. To do that, I had to forgive and pray for him. The Holy Spirit told me that when he sees me again, he will see *Him*. I didn't understand what God was talking about.

The Holy Spirit said it again, "Sherrie, he will only see *Me!*"

Time passed, and again he got in touch with me by phone at my workplace. He shared with me that he had been dealing with an illness and was legally blind in both eyes for the past couple of years. He was able to hear the Holy Spirit and love of God in me instead of seeing my outer appearance. He apologized for all the harmful and hurtful things he did to me. I accepted and appreciated his apology. I apologized to him for the pain I caused about the paternity of my daughter. Before he passed away at the age of 42, we shared our different testimonies about how giving our lives to Christ changed our lives. He told me that he really loved me, I didn't deserve to be treated that way, and wished he could redo his life.

I said to him, "Keep moving forward with Christ and make every minute count."

I knew then what Holy Spirit meant when He said to me, "He will on see *Him!*"

My abuser became my brother is Christ. He began to share how God gave him another chance to truly love someone else and how blessed he was to have that opportunity. He shared how good God had been to him by allowing him to truly love and appreciate who he had left in his life. He also shared how grateful he was I took his call, which was the last time we got to talk. We truly forgave each other. We were young, and no matter how bad it was, God gave both of us a chance to grow and change. My brother-in-Christ is totally free and forgiven. Because of our change in relationship, I went to his mother's funeral to pay my respects. I was able to share the love of God with his family members too.

I thought the memory of this chapter in my life was completely over. The pain resurfaced in my mind again, mixed with the death of my daddy. I couldn't shake off this cycle until I truly started receiving in my heart the love God has for me and that my life wasn't over. The devil is behind the thoughts of the pain. The devil only knows your past. He has no clue about your future. Everyone can receive forgiveness and love from Father God. Therefore, it's important for us to renew our mind and believe that we are loved, forgiven, and precious to God. Jesus paid the price for everyone even if you don't receive Him. It's never too late to be forgiven. God truly gave me His beauty from ashes!

Isaiah 61:3 (NKJV) states, "To console those who mourn in Zion, To give them beauty for ashes, The oil of joy for mourning, The garment of praise for the spirit of heaviness; That they may be called trees of righteousness, The planting of the LORD, that He may be glorified."

-

Even though you may feel angry after reading this chapter, he is free and accepted in the beloved arms of God. He has nothing else to do with how I felt and the trauma I was still managing. One thing I want everyone to walk away with is to please check on your mom, sisters, daughters, nieces, and any woman you may know that you suspect is being abused. Out of fear, they may be too afraid to share. It's a cycle that slowly starts and grows into an aggressive behavior that can cause death to the victim. Please hear my heart.

Chapter 9

THE GENTLEMAN

"Marriage is honorable in all, and the bed undefined: but whoremongers and adulterers God will judge!"

- Hebrews 13:4

Put your rocks, bricks, and hammers down! Too many men and woman in the body of Christ and in world are dealing with guilt, shame, and depression for choices they made. Women have shared that they have been abused or their husband or baby daddy left them for another woman. Those testimonies are heartfelt, and they are given so much grace, mercy, and sympathy. How often can a woman or man who committed the very act of adultery, abuse, or cheating can confess their faults and receive the same grace, mercy, and sympathy? It rarely happens. I've heard countless of stories about infidelity and adultery. From the beginning starting with Eve, the first woman, many accused her of Adam's fall. She played a part in the fall of the first man, but God gave the instructions to Adam. Read Genesis chapter 3. For my sisters-in-Christ that have or are currently dealing with drug abuse and your addiction caused you to do some shameful acts to support your addiction, good news, Jesus loves and died for you too. God knows you are out there. For my sisters-in-Christ that are currently in a relationship with someone's husband, boyfriend, or just accepting less than God's best, Jesus loves and died for you too. God knows you are out there! I've been there when I willingly shared my husband. It was a mental and physical stronghold...but God! Yes, this is still happening in the church and the world today. For my sisters-in-Christ that have been delivered from the lifestyle, but still have a residue of shame, are dealing with people that are mentally condemning you, and you are torturing yourself, Jesus loves and died for you too. God knows you are out there! For my sisters-in-Christ that willingly slept with her mother's husband, may have a baby by him too, and are reminded of the mistake you made every time you look at your child, Jesus loves and died for you too. The child has a purpose and is still a gift. God knows you are out there! For my sisters-in-Christ that slept with her sister's friend or family member's husband or boyfriend, Jesus loves and died for you too. God knows you are out there! For my sisters-in-Christ that are being called into the body of Christ and currently sharing a man, I pray you have a change of heart. You know in your heart you are being called. Your first step is to come as you are to Christ, receive Him, His Love, and the price He paid for you on Calvary. God knows you are out there!

Everyone deserves forgiveness. Just like Jesus did for the woman who was caught committing adultery in the Scripture (John 8:1-11 KJV). Read and absorb Jesus' words to her in verse 11:

"Jesus went unto the mount of Olives. And early in the morning he came again into the temple, and all the people came unto him; and he sat down, and taught them. And the scribes and Pharisees brought unto him a woman taken in adultery; and when they had set her in the midst, they say unto him, Master, this woman was taken in adultery, in the very act. Now Moses in the law commanded us, that such should be stoned: but what sayest thou? This they said, tempting him, that they might have to accuse him. But Jesus stooped down, and with his finger wrote on the ground, as though he heard them not. So when they continued asking him, he lifted up himself, and said unto them, He that is without sin among you, let him first cast a stone at her. And again he stooped down, and wrote on the ground. And they which heard it, being convicted by their own conscience, went out one by one, beginning at the eldest, even unto the last: and Jesus was left alone, and the woman standing in the midst. When Jesus had lifted up himself, and saw none but the woman, he said unto her, Woman, where are those thine accusers? hath no man condemned thee? She said, No man, Lord. And Jesus said unto her, Neither do I condemn thee: go, and sin no more."

You must *sin no more*! God has forgiven many shameful women as the woman with the alabaster box (Luke 7:36 – 50). She washed Jesus' feet with her tears and wiped them away with her hair. She anointed him with the fine fragrance in her alabaster box. She gave him her best. You are God's best. Give Him your pain and shame.

For my sisters-in-Christ that have been hurt by our sisters-in-Christ described above, God knows you are out there! My sister, you are fearfully and wonderfully made just like the Bible states in Psalm 139:14. No matter the hurt and embarrassment you may have felt or are still feeling, God brought you out because that man has always cheated on you. He wasn't yours alone, you never had him to yourself. He cheated during your entire relationship. You are free. If you chose to stay in your marriage, you are not stupid or crazy for fighting for your marriage. Learn

God's way of fighting, in prayer not in the flesh. As you read this chapter, I pray you will see how God brought me through. Willingly, I shared my husband with the understanding that he was torn. While trying to grasp it, I was being called to obey God. Either way, it was going to cause a lot of heartache.

More women commit adultery than men. How can I say this? I can because I lived it. One man can have multiple women that accept his poor behavior. In most cases, we know what's going on. We can feel it without evidence. When you're young and without a relationship with God, it feels like you are on top of the world. Sex feels good. Being lusted after is appealing to a woman who can't see her worth; only what her body can offer. Some infidelity just runs in a family. The worst part about it is no one can discuss it. Some women will stay with a man because they must have him. Women will fight and blame each other and blame his family for allowing him to cheat. They have a heap of other reasons except for the main cause, which is that we don't know who we genuinely are. When you look in the mirror and become the other woman that's hurting, you wouldn't do it. I dealt with being cheated on and I was one who cheated with someone who was in a committed relationship. He wasn't married.

In Proverbs 21:9 (KJV), it reads, "It is better to dwell in a corner of the housetop, than with a brawling woman in a wide house." In another version (NIV) it states, "Better to live on a corner of the roof than share a house with a quarrelsome wife." Both clearly state that a wife can be quarrelsome, brawling, and nagging, and that the man is better off by himself. Most woman become the roof top. In so many cases, the grass does look greener on the other side, especially when dealing with a nagging woman. The other side is lust, soft music, a beautiful face, or a sexy body. It is also appealing clothing, a nicer atmosphere, someone to talk to, bubble bath, trips, massages, back rubs, and whatever makes him feels better than being at home. I have spoken to men that have complained about their wives, girlfriends, and baby mamas, saying they didn't support their dreams or visions. Whatever the case may be, it's not for another woman to become the roof top in a marriage or committed relationship, no matter how bad things are. Now, some women have taken that good husband, baby daddy, or boyfriend for granted because they thought they had him wrapped around their finger. Trust me, it's always another woman who will appreciate your good man and love him the way you should've loved him. If you keep up this behavior and continue to use and abuse that good man, he will leave and not return. Learn to appreciate your good man if you have one. On another note, no matter what the wife did or is doing in their relationship, if you know he's married, it's not your place to make things worse. The lyrics to "If I Was Your Woman" seems good, but if acted on, it leads to destruction. If he's married or living with someone, it's not God's best for His daughters.

Some women are living in pain trying to hold to an image based on having a big house, nice cars, and trips, yet they are sleeping in separate bedrooms. Peace does not exist in the house. I have seen women look twenty years younger once they got out of those bad marriages and relationships. They looked refreshed and healed. They started taking care of their health, physical and emotional wellbeing, with the understanding that they deserve better. As a believer in Christ, we have a way out if we want it. Ask God to create in you a clean heart as state in Psalms 51:10 (NLT), "Create in me a clean heart, O God. Renew a loyal spirit within me. Know your worth. Seek to know your worth with everything that's in you. Romans 2:23-2 4 (NLT) reads, "For everyone has sinned; we all fall short of God's glorious standard. Yet God, in his grace, freely makes us right in his sight. He did this through Christ Jesus when he freed us from the penalty for our sins." Change the music in your story. I did!

-

My Story My Testimony

Coming up in the early 70's and 80's, I was a nosey little girl, always alert. The writers of the music said it all. I listened to the lyrics and watched the actions of adults. When a song was played, I knew right off the jump what it was about. The songs were about someone who was in love, cheating, hurting, or overall, just ready to dance. I was four years old in 1972. I loved how one of my aunts and her husband danced and kissed each other off a song by Al Green called "I've Never Found a Girl." If that song was played 10 times, they still danced and held each other like they were so in love. I said that when I got big, I was going to dance like with my husband. I loved hanging out with my daddy and his side of the family. They were a lot of fun and had a lot of action. Plenty of interesting people were in our presence during those card games. From time to time, when a certain record was played, I was able to tell what it meant and what was about to go down. One day at one of those card games, someone repeatedly played a song. A friend of the family was bent over with his head in his hands while patting his feet to the beat. I was eight years old when that record came out. The man looked confused, like he didn't know what to do. His wife suddenly became mad at him.

She said, "All you have to do is pick one!"

Then she broke the record in half. The song was "Tyrin' To Love Two" by William Bell (1977). I laughed, not knowing the pain behind the scenes. Years later while visiting, the same couple got into an argument again over another record called "I Rather Be by Myself" by Ebo. The husband sung that song like he meant every word.

The wife said to her husband, "Get the f*** out and go be by yourself!"

She put him out my uncle's house, but years later, they were still together, still fighting to stay together. On another occasion another song was played "I'll be the Other Woman" by The Soul Children. A lady who was visiting proudly sang that song like it was the National Anthem. She wanted it played repeatedly, and each time she sang it louder with more body language—the lifting of her hands beating on her chest. That song was her jam! All the women loved another song that was played. They danced and sometimes cried at the same time to "Young Hearts Run Free" by Candi Station. To seal the deal for me, at the age 17, the song "I Have Learned to Respect the Power of Love" by Stephanie Mills came out. I played that song often, not understanding the true meaning. Fast forward to 2007, I watched *Why Did I Get Married* by Tyler Perry in the movie theater and saw part of my story. It was unbelievablc. I must admit, I was the character Angela in so many ways. Never in a million years did I expect those four songs to be part of my adult life story.

Early July of 1990, at the age of 21, I was visiting one of my best friends. We have been friends since 1979. As we sat on the pouch reminiscing about childhood, a gentleman was standing afar. She knew him. I didn't. We had this *secret* game we played. We said the opposite of what we meant. For example, when I was hot, I said I was cold. I asked her who that sexy man was. He was not attractive at all to me. My friend went to speak to him for a minute.

When she returned, she said, "I told him you liked him!"

"Wait! What the what?"

She lied. My friend said that he was nice and was better than the one who was abusing me at that time. "No way. That gentleman was a bamma," I thought. He was 11 years older than me. He was different than what I was used to. I thought he looked like a Caribbean singer. We immediately started calling him Bill. Two weeks passed and I returned to my old neighborhood to see my friend again. We were headed to the corner store and Bill pulled up in his car. He called my friend and they talked for a minute. She returned and told me that Bill wanted her to give me his beeper number. "No way," I thought. I took the number, but I didn't page Bill until July 23, 1990.

Why Didn't He Run When He Had a Chance?

I was not mentally ready for a relationship. I didn't properly heal from the abusive one. I didn't have a relationship with Christ. I was still lost! I frequently asked why Bill didn't run for his life! Bill ignored all the warning signs! When we met, I was told up front by him that he was not married and not to get attached. I was 21 years old and trying to get out of an abusive relationship.

"First of all, who's to say you're not going to get attached to me!" I responded.

I felt quite insulted by Bill saying that to me. Neither one of us thought it would last. I took what I could get. At the time Bill, was involved with multiple women, all at once. I became involved with him too. Eventually, we began to spend a lot of time together every day. Three warning signs were given. Bill had a chance to get away from the broken woman I was. The first sign to run was when Bill encountered my abuser, which could have been deadly. I thought I was going to become homeless.

Immediately, Bill made sure I had a place to stay. My abuser harassed me for a while. Bill was not afraid of him. Five months later, on New Year's Eve, to keep a promise I made three years prior, I told a lie to Bill. I was wearing my Christmas gift he brought me. It was a beautiful leather and fox collar coat. Bill was taking me to the store. I looked to my left and couldn't believe who I saw.

"Stop the car and let me out. I've been waiting for three long years to see my *friend*."

I was so excited. Bill pulled over, not knowing what was about to happen. I went to keep a promise I made, and I did just that. At least I thought I was. By no means was she a friend! While fighting, my coat was ripped and wet because we fell in the snow. Sitting back in his car, Bill was shocked, confused, and couldn't believe what he saw. He got out of the car to come and get me.

I said, "Hey I've been waiting, and I knew you wouldn't have stopped." All I could say was, "I'm sorry."

Bill looked like he saw the devil...speechless. Even after thirty-one years together, Bill is still traumatized. Whenever I say someone is my friend, he is reminded of that moment. The third warning came a few months later when Bill taught me how to drive. Two days after getting my license, I wrecked his brand-new car. I didn't stop at the stop sign and I hit another car. Bill came back to my apartment to talk about the accident, but I went skating and had a good time. I wanted to make sure I didn't have any broken bones. I thought it was no big deal. Bill was astonished, wondering what kind of girl he was dating. Yes, girl, not a woman. Bill was a peaceful person. In dealing with me, I sometimes put him into situations that he wasn't used to. Because he was so kind, I would have fought a man if they bothered Bill. He preferred to walk away. In one incident at the corner store near my home, the store clerk verbally assaulted Bill.

He said, "You are too old to have that young lady."

"What did you say? Baby, punch him in the face," I countered.

"I'm not paying that fool no mind," Bill stated and walked out of the store.

I was angry and went back to the store later. I confronted the clerk with some harsh words to let him know not to insult my man.

When you know something up front, you have the chance to decide whether to stay or jump ship. Bill was just so nice and peaceful, it seemed unreal. What I loved about him the most was the love he had for his mother, sisters, and nieces. He took care of them and would have done anything for them. We talked for hours about the love he had for them. Loving Bill came easy. I didn't care about the other women. I got 99% of his time. I shared what was going on with one of my favorite cousins who I could talk to about anything.

She said, "I'm telling you. You going to get attached and your feelings will change. Get out of that relationship now!"

My aunt, her mother, interjected, "Girl, don't you let that good man go! He's nice and taking care of you. What are you going to do? Go get a broke cheater? I don't think so. Girl, keep that good man!"

While smoking her joint, my aunt laughed. We all laughed!

It happened a year later. I was attached! I was given the best and the worst advice at the same time. My abuser often criticized me for leaving him to date Bill. He didn't have muscles or a six pack like my abuser, but what Bill did have was much better. We were five years into our relationship when I lost my dad. My world was all over the place. The morning Bill came to see me, I told him that my dad had died six hours ago. He didn't know what to do. I needed Bill to just hold me. We both were in our birthday suits.

"My daddy just died, and this is how you comfort me. Is this all you can think about?"

It was totally disrespectful, but good at the same time. To me, everything was going well in our relationship. I didn't focus on anything else but our relationship and spending time with Bill. In 1997, we decided to get married. We were not serving or living a Christian life. We didn't seek God before saying I do. I was the wife and the side chick at the same time. I was still cool with the terms.

In 1998, I gave my life to Christ and joined a church. I quickly ended that church membership, but I still wanted to know more about being in Christ. I was invited to another church closer to my home. Broken, depressed, confused, and suicidal, I came as I was along with my daughter into the ministry. Within weeks, my daughter and I were baptized on the same day. I was ready and fully persuaded to live for Christ. I still had the mindset that I didn't belong, and God didn't want a person like me. Lies of the enemy played in my mind daily. I continued to cry, sob, and ask God to help me. The more I submitted to God, the more things were exposed to me before my eyes. God showed me everything that was displeasing to Him. I knew the difference between displeasing and condemnation, which is from the devil and others. The conviction was God's love for me. Proverbs 3:11 states, "My son, despise not the chastening of the LORD; neither be weary of his correction." I wasn't accountable for what

I didn't know. Once I knew, I was absolutely accountable. My eyes began to open in the Spirit. The Holy Spirit is my helper. It's that still, small voicc in my heart.

-

I remember the Holy Spirit asking me a few questions. Scriptures were not given; it was just a conversation. I really didn't want to put in this book the conversation because I was ashamed that I did that very act and I preferred to take it to my grave. At the time I did this I was 22 years old.

"How would I feel if another woman slept in your bed while you were out of town?" the Holy Spirit probed.

"I would cut his throat!"

No, I did not have sex in that home, but I was there on a regular.

The Holy Spirit said that we must share it because so many of God's daughters are still doing this very thing and it could be deadly if this behavior continues in their lives. The Holy Spirit wants to bring conviction, not shame, only deliverance. Over the last several years in the Washington, D.C. metropolitan area, there have been so many murders of women, their family members, and their children due to one person having a relationship with a married man or in a committed relationship. The stress of being caught has caused the men to mentally erupt and murder to keep from being exposed.

The Holy Spirit asked me back in the year 2000, "Sherrie, how would feel if your husband brought another woman into your home?"

I responded, "I would kill a b****!"

Yes, I was a cussing Christian. Back then, ten out ten words were a curse word.

The Holy Spirit then asked, "How would you feel if your husband pulled up driving the other woman's car to your home?"

"I would bust the windows out."

"Then stay out of that other home!"

I saw if the tables were the other way, I wouldn't have liked it at all. I received my correction. My sisters, if you are doing this, please look at it a different way. I knew so many women that were constantly dealing with their baby-daddy or husband cheating on them. I watched some of my dearest friends go through the same thing that I was willingly doing. I watched the fist fights between women, tears, and embarrassment when thinking the man was committed. Someone else's misfortune was not a platform to dance on. It wasn't an issue for me because I was the wife and chick on side at the same time in my marriage. Once I dedicated my life to God, it was an issue for my God. God began to show me that it wasn't the best for me, or anyone affected by my actions. I took full responsibility. Change was coming.

My sisters, the man that God has for you will not look like what you had. It will be totally opposite. Have you overlooked your Boaz? Bill is my husband. We've been together for 31 years. By the way, he hates being called Bill.

If You Give It Up, You Can Have It All!

"Seeing ye have purified your souls in obeying the truth through the Spirit unto unfeigned love of the brethren, see that ye love one another with a pure heart fervently," states 1 Peter 1:22 (KJV). Giving up something or someone you love is not easy! Letting go or losing someone is the most devastating thing a human could ever bare. Losing a job, house, car, or any other material thing can be replaced. Even still, some have killed themselves over material things. When you lose another human, the residue of the heartache can affect many lives, all at once. In contrast, when you give up something for God, you will not lose. You only gain.

Every Sunday at church I heard something about marriage. My pastors are big on marriages and spouses honoring each other. I saw how they honored each other and have a passion for marriages and family. It was no way possible to be under their great leadership and not change and want better for my household. Some of my family members were clueless about my marriage. My daughter only knew was that I was happy. She didn't see my husband hit me. One Sunday while at church, our assistant pastor made a big statement in his sermon.

He said, "I wish someone would invite me somewhere and my wife couldn't come! We are a package deal!"

It did something on the inside of me. God began to show the hurt and pain I was feeling. I then realized the hurt and pain I caused. That was not God's best for neither of us. We didn't want to make the first move. Irrespective of the outcome, someone was going to emotionally get hurt.

God began to speak to me about saving the lost.

God said, "I need you to go after them with your whole heart."

I didn't think about it starting at my own front door. Everyone around me knew that God was doing a work in me. I no longer wanted to share my husband, not even with me...the side chick. I was loving who I was becoming.

I had a talk with my husband about his salvation and rededicating his life to the Lord. I began to share what the Lord was showing me that displeased Him. I told him I had been praying and I had asked God to remove me if I wasn't who he was supposed to spend the rest of his life with. It was easy to place the responsibility in God's hand. It was my responsibility to remove myself. I shared with my husband that I loved him so much, and to let him go, it was no longer about us, but God. Infidelity would no longer to be accepted, no matter how many years we had together. God began to show me how we were hurting so many in our family. They didn't have a say in our choices. The infidelity was kept away from my family and most of my friends. They only knew we were always together, happy, and we took care of each other.

I was asked by one of my husband's family members, "Why all of sudden the change now?"

"This is not God's best for me or anyone in this dysfunctional marriage," I answered.

His family was living around his lifestyle and choices far too long. They needed to be set free as well.

As I looked back over my childhood and the card games my family had, I realized that the women who were involved with the same man were in the same room. Even in my parent's home at their card games, women that were sleeping with my father were in our home, laughing and eating my mother's food. Unfortunately, it is condoned in too many families. Infidelity is embraced as normal. My mother didn't allow any of our family members, mainly her brother and sisters-in-law, to bring outside relationships in our home when they were married. My mom didn't tolerate the disrespect. On the other hand, it was normal on my dad's side of the family. Some had the husband, wife, girlfriends, and boyfriends together at the family functions...having fun without a clue. It was called the Player's Card! When I went to bed, my dad was home. When I woke up, he was leaving for work. My childhood became a reality in my adult life. I had to change the music!

God shared with me that I had to transform the way I was seeing, thinking, and speaking. I had to learn how to pray heartfelt prayers for my husband. I began to look in the Scriptures concerning myself in my husband life. The Scripture that spoke to my heart the most was Proverbs 31:11-12, which read, "The heart of her husband doth safely trust in her so that he shall have no need of spoil, she will do him good and not evil all the days of her life." I began to pray for my husband and intercede on his behalf. I prayed for him to hear God's voice. I prayed for God to convict his heart. I prayed for God to reveal, expose, and remove everyone that didn't have my husband's best interest at heart. I prayed for God to tear down anything in my husband's life that did not bring Him glory. That tearing down brought out those that were abusing his kindness. I prayed for his mind, his health, and soul. I prayed for God to remove any condemnation about his past. I prayed for God to use my husband for His glory. I prayed that my husband loved me like Christ loved the church. In Ephesians 5:25 and Colossians 3:19, the Word says for husbands to love their wives and be not bitter against them. I truly accepted that no matter what, if my husband chose to stay in our union or leave, either way I was good...indeed good. I understood who I was in Christ! Once God began to remove everything that didn't bring Him Glory, the devil came for my mind, telling me that I was stuck with the bill. The devil tortured me with the thoughts that my husband was no good. What God did with those prayers I was praying over my husband was that He answered those heartfelt prayers like in James 5:16 (KJV): "Confess your faults one to another, that ye may be healed. The effectual fervent prayer of a righteous man availeth much." Those prayers drew my husband to rededicate his life to Christ. Those prayers removed the stress and pressure on my husband's heart and body. Those prayers prolonged my husband's life. Those prayers gave my husband restful nights and released burdens placed on him from taking care of many adults. God gave my husband another chance to truly love me like he was supposed to do.

I had peace. I knew that when I did the right thing and took the high road, God covered me. Ten years later, I understood what my first lady said to me.

"If you give it up, you can have it all!"

God showed me that I was good either way with the outcome because He had me! My release came easy when it was done in God's strength. I do understand that I have a blended family, and I must keep my heart right. The other parents of our children are still a part of our family. My husband and I had to come to a mutual ground and respect the choice that was made. I stay in a position of prayer and ready to have the agape love for everyone in my blended family. I gave the Holy Spirit, who is my helper, permission to lead and guide me. I do my best to accept and be at peace with my blended family. Because of the love I have for our children, I embrace their mothers and fathers too. At some point in our lives, we will come together for celebrations and in times of mourning. My husband and I truly loved the Lord, and we are in constant prayer for our children, grandchildren, family, and friends.

Chapter 10
LEGAL MURDERS

"I acknowledge my sin unto thee, and mine iniquity
have I not hid. I said, I will confess my transgressions
unto the LORD; and thou forgavest the iniquity
of my sin. Selah."

- Psalm 32:5

On July 22, 1991, while watching the news, a breaking news headliner at the bottom of the screen showed that a serial killer was caught. He murdered several people and hid their body parts in the freezer. It was later stated that he ate some of the body parts. I thought to myself that they need to pull out the electric chair again. Four years later, while grieving over my dad's death and reliving the memories from my abusive relationship, the devil dug up my abortions.

I heard another voice say, "I dare you think and talked about my Jeffrey like that."

Who the heck is Jeffrey? Jeffrey Dahmer. His story resurfaced in the news headline.

That voice said to me, "What's the difference between you and him? The only difference is that you didn't eat them! You did allow them to be grinded in that vacuum!

You weren't mentally disturbed. You willingly had your babies killed! My Jeffery was mentally ill! You thought because your government made it lawful to abort those babies with no jail time you could. Your God said otherwise! Didn't your Bible tell you in the commandments, 'Thou shall not kill?' Sherrie, you murdered those babies!"

I now know that was the voice of the devil. He is the accuser of the brethren. He is the father of lies! He will use half-truths to accuse you! Of my hardships, this is the most devastating. To this day, I wish I could undo what I did after giving my life to Christ. Yes, I had several abortions before I knew the Lord. I truly felt like at eight weeks the babies were just blood in my stomach and by aborting them, I wasn't killing a child. Those abortions were my most kept secret. I hid my transgressions from my family and everyone else except the two men who didn't want me to have my babies. I know there are a lot of women in the body of Christ or in general that are still dealing with guilt and shame for making the same decision. Let me uncover my mask. I have repented for those acts every day and still felt like I wasn't forgiven. I had thoughts telling me that the only way to make it right with God was to kill myself. I couldn't shake the thoughts that kept telling I was a murderer. When I saw women come up for prayer in church to conceive a baby, that voice reminded me how I aborted my babies. That voice reminded me of the vacuum and tubes connected to the machine. I repeatedly heard in my mind that I was a murderer.

God shared with me that many of His daughters are having or had the guilt over their heads for many years as I. For 32 years, I lived with guilt and shame. Every time I see a baby or a woman with a lot of children, I'm reminded of my babies I didn't keep. It doesn't matter if you had one, two, three, or ten abortions. You can be forgiven and set free of the guilt and shame. True repentance is not only confession, but it is going in the opposite direction and not committing that sin or look that way again. Beating yourself up for something that's already done that you can't undo will never make it go away. The only way is to receive that Jesus paid the price for your sins and you are forgiven. Turn that shame into something positive by helping others not to abort their babies. It's plenty of families and people who would love children as their own. Consider adoption if you cannot raise your child.

I made those choices to abort my babies without having the understanding that the fruit of the womb is blessed. Psalm 127:3-5 states, "Lo, children are an heritage of the LORD: and the fruit of the womb is his reward. As arrows are in the hand of a mighty man; so are children of the youth. Happy is the man that hath his quiver full of them: they shall not be ashamed, but they shall speak with the enemies in the gate." We are forgiven, we are loved, we are free to give and love children all over this world, in our families, our neighbor's children, and the children you may have now. Receive your forgiveness!

To my sisters in Christ and women who are having challenges conceiving, I apologize to you if this chapter in my life brings you any type of heartache. My prayer for you is you shall conceive in Jesus' name! Continue to have faith in God and trust that He hears your heartfelt prayer. Your child may come to you from another mother, God knows you will love and care for that child and be the mother He knows you are.

Below are the Scriptures that I had to get deep down in my heart, but first in my mind to be released from the guilt and shame that caused me to be oppressed for years:

"Confess your faults one to another, that ye may be healed. The effectual fervent prayer of a righteous man avail much." (James 5:16)

"Therefore if any man be in Christ, he is a new creature: old things are passed away; behold, all things are become new." (2 Corinthians 5:17)

"The Lord is a stronghold of the oppressed, a stronghold in the times of trouble." (Psalm 9:9, NLT)

"There is therefore now no condemnation for those who are in Christ Jesus." (Romans 8:1, NLT)

I repeat...it doesn't matter if you had one, two, three, or ten abortions. You can be forgiven and set free of the guilt. True repentance is never committing the same act ever again in life.

I asked God how I can be used in the kingdom with this chapter in my life. I know many in the faith have been fighting for years to seek change in our nation to abolish the rights to have an abortion with no prevail. God is bigger than our government, and with the boldness God has given me, I can and will be a voice in the movement to anyone that will listen. Thank you, Jesus, for paying the price for me on Calvary, for dying for me, and for shedding your blood for my sins! Thank you for putting me in right-standing with God the father.

Chapter 11

WRESTLE NOT

"For we wrestle not against flesh and blood, but against principalities, against powers, against the rules of the darkness of this world, against spiritual wickedness in high places."

- Ephesians 6:12, KJV

Choosing our friends is a wonderful gift that God has given us. We didn't have a say in the family we were born into. To meet and grow with others outside of our immediate family is an amazing journey. It can also be hurtful and sometimes devastating to end those friendships. For years, despite having some wonderful friends in my life, I clung more to the hurtful friendships. Most of my energy was given to those that I knew didn't like me. Every chance they got I was shown that I didn't matter. I was only appreciated when they were benefiting from me. Out the kindness of my heart, I didn't hold back anything they needed. Those spiteful people caused a lot of strain on others who were mutual friends with the parties involved. It made it difficult for the shared friends to show loyalty to both. It came a time when some had to remove themselves to have a peace of mind. Some mutual friends contributed to the damaging behaviors. Others matured over time and began to stand for what was right, which was difficult to do. Despite our hurtful friendships, our parents loved all of us as their own. Tragedy and hardships hit our families and we lost loved ones. Because of those heartbreaks, we put aside petty arguments and came together to help each other through those hard times.

At work, I was in relationships with people I had no business being friends with; those that had a relationship with Christ. Most were Christians hurting Christians in the workplace. I was surprised by the envy and jealousy. Some didn't want others to get ahead or weren't happy for a co-worker's success. The relationships ended with unforgiveness and bitterness. It was upsetting to experience betrayal among my brothers and sisters in Christ in the workplace. I changed my mindset about the workplace after I read one book. I had to make corrections in many ways. I learned how I created some of the behaviors in the workplace as well. I often refer to that book when I need help in the managing work. *The Ten Commandments for Working in Hostile Environment* by Bishop T. D. Jakes, who also taught a message on this topic. It was life changing for me. Colossians 3:23-24

(KJV) states, "And whatsoever ye do, do it heartily, as to the Lord, and not unto men; Knowing that of the Lord ye shall receive the reward of the inheritance: for ye serve the Lord Christ." I used this Scripture to clear up and remove the feelings I had to please people and from thinking people were my source for increase and promotion in the workplace.

I hung around people that I knew were stabbing me in my back and not happy for me. Everyone around me saw that those manipulating friendships were not good for my wellbeing. Those individuals were not people I should've called friends. I'm in 30 years or more deep, still trying to put those fallen apples back on my tree to grow and connect. I badly wanted to be accepted by them, but I was running on empty. I had nothing else to give. I temporarily broke off for a while, but then I went back, and the vicious cycle continued. One two-letter word that I often overlooked in forgiving those individuals was "if". Those individuals didn't repent or acknowledge the offenses or treatments toward me. I forgave without holding them accountable. According to Scripture, they should have acknowledged their sins and asked for forgiveness. In Luke 17:3-4 KJV, it states, "Take heed to yourselves: If thy brother trespass against thee, rebuke him; and if he repent, forgive him. And if he trespass against thee seven times in a day, and seven times in a day turn again to thee, saying, I repent; thou shalt forgive him."

Have you seen a pattern when you allowed a person to keep hurting you without them acknowledging their offense? The Word of God instructs us as to confess our faults to one another. James 5:16 says, "Confess your faults one to another, and pray one for another, that ye may be healed. The effectual fervent prayer of a righteous man availeth much." 1 John 1:9 states, "If we confess our sins, he is faithful and just to forgive us our sins, and to cleanse us from all unrighteousness." Now, what if the person doesn't repent. God gave us a Word for that in Ephesians 4:31-32 (NIV), which reads, "Get rid of all bitterness, rage and anger, brawling and slander, along with every form of malice. Be kind and compassionate to one another, forgiving each other, just as in Christ God forgave you.

One day, I reviewed Scriptures about friendship. I always heard Proverbs 18:24a (NKJV), which reads, "A man *who has* friends must himself be friendly." I thought I was doing it. I used what I learned in the Scriptures below to break the stronghold to stay connected to those individuals that weren't good for me.

- Psalm 109:4 (NIV): "In return for my friendship they accuse me, but I am a woman of prayer."
- Psalm 109:5 (NIV): "They repay me evil for good, and hatred for my friendship."
- Proverbs 16:28 (NIV): "A perverse person stirs up conflict, and a gossip separates close friends."
- 1 Corinthians 15:33 (NIV): "Do not be misled: Bad Company corrupts good character."
- Proverbs 22:24 (NIV): "Do not make friends with a hot-tempered person, do not associate with one easily angered."

I held onto those friendships that had the characteristics described in the above Scriptures. None of them loved me *at all times*. Proverbs 17:17a (NIV) states, "A friend loves at all times." I had to look on the inside of myself and find the root cause of the desire to cling and remain connected to those relationships. I was dealing with the fear of rejection. I had a people-pleasing spirit. I wasted too much of my time. Because of my fear, I lacked peace and couldn't move on. No one wants to be rejected. I asked God to show me anyone I was rejecting. God showed me that I disregarded my family and the people that were my true friends, those that loved me and wanted to spend time with me. They have been there for me and loved being in my presence. My true friends are never demanding nor forceful with our time. We picked up where we left off. I felt full and renewed when I was with them.

I also rejected potential new friendships God had in mind for my future. For years, I gave my loyalty to people that were not my friends. I asked God to help me to dig up the roots of the strongholds in those abusive friendships. One thing I had to do was to stop describing those individuals as my sisters and friends. According to the Scriptures, they were not. I also needed to acknowledge that as much as I wanted them to be my friends, I wasn't a friend to them either. I outwardly showed love and support, but I had to check my heart. Because of how they treated me, I was happy when they suffered heartaches and trials in their lives. In my mind, their suffering was payback for all the pain they caused and the hatred they had for me. Unknowingly, I was misusing what the Bible says about vengeance. I misused the Scriptures concerning how God dealt with my enemies who spitefully used me. God instructions were for the believer to bless your enemies and do good. Matthew 5:44 (NKJV) states, "But I say to you, love your enemies, bless those who curse you, do good to those who hate you, and pray for those who spitefully use you and persecute you." How can someone be a friend and an enemy? It happens all the time.

I had to repent and ask God to forgive me, cleanse my heart, uproot all bitterness, anger, strife, and unknown jealousy in my heart. Why would I mention jealousy? I wasn't jealous of anyone. Jealousy is anything you feel that another person doesn't deserve, no matter who they are. Yes, jealousy had to be removed from my heart. I had resentment toward some in the workplace. I watched people beat the system while I was working with my hands earning an honest living. I watched people in the workplace take the credit for my hard work. I was jealous and angry at the same time.

I wanted understanding. I wanted freedom. I wanted to be free. So, I began to pray. I began to forgive and began to look beyond the natural and look in spirit. That was a spiritual fight. I had to end the fleshly fight. I began to pray for release from the relationships and all strongholds. I had to fight my desire to stay connected to those individuals. I began to pray for them and asked God to heal their hearts and bless them. I needed to ingrain these Scriptures in my heart and mind:

- 2 Chronicles 7:14 (NIV): "If my people who are called by my name, will humble themselves and pray and seek my face and turn from their wicked ways, then I will hear from heaven, and I will forgive their sin and will heal their land. Lord help me to humble, pray, seek, and turn from any wicked ways."

- 2 Corinthians 5:17: "Therefore, if anyone is in Christ, he is a new creature. The old has passed away, behold the new has come. I'm a new creature in Christ.

- Romans 15:7 (NIV): "Accept one another, then just as Christ accepted you, in order to bring praise to God. I chose to accept others just as Christ accepted me in my shortcomings."

- Philippians 2:13 (NLT): "God is working in you, giving you the desire and the power to do what pleases Him. I want a Heart that cares."

- Romans 12:18 (NIV): "If it is possible as far as it depends on you live at peace with everyone. Lord help me to live at peace with everyone."

I love how God helped me to overcome the spirit of fear of rejection and has truly given me an open space. I no longer desire to be part of a small circle of friends. In any circle, no one can get out or get in. Being in an open space gives me the power to receive and let go without the fear of rejection. I so appreciate the gift from God that allows us to choose our friends and I will not take my friends or future friends for granted ever again.

GRATEFUL

Thankfulness and Prayer

"I thank my God upon every remembrance of you, always in every prayer of mine making request for you all with joy, for your fellowship in the gospel from the first day until now, being confident of this very thing, that He who has begun a good work in you will complete it until the day of Jesus Christ; just as it is right for me to think this of you all, because I have you in my heart, inasmuch as both in my chains and in the defense and confirmation of the gospel, you all are partakers with me of grace. For God is my witness, how greatly I long for you all with the affection of Jesus Christ. And this I pray, that your love may abound still more and more in knowledge and all discernment, that you may approve the things that are excellent, that you may be sincere and without offense till the day of Christ, being filled with the fruits of righteousness which are by Jesus Christ, to the glory and praise of God."

- Philippians 1:3-11 (NKJV)

Chapter 12

APPRECIATING WHO I HAVE LEFT IN MY LIFE

And God will generously provide all you need. Then you will always have everything you need and plenty left over to share with other.

- 2 Corinthians 9:8 (NLT)

In life, it is too easy to get comfortable with who and what we have in our lives. We find out how precious it was when it's taken away. One day, I was having a conversation with the Holy Spirit. No Scriptures were given to me, and it was just a clear conversation with plenty of heartfelt revelation. I asked the Holy Spirit why I cried buckets of tears for weeks when Michael Jackson and Whitney Huston died. I grew up listening to their music and talent, but I didn't meet them in person. When two of Washington, D.C.'s icons in the Go-Go music arena died, I didn't cry. I celebrated and played their music. I met them in person. I wanted to cry. I tried to make myself cry, but not one tear fell. I asked the Holy Spirt what was the difference. The revelation was that I didn't appreciate the gifts. Michael Jackson and Whitney Huston were gifts from God. Then Holy Spirit said that I made fun of their gifts. I took them for granted. I made fun of their trials and tribulations. When they were taken away, I realized how valuable they were.

"Now you know they did and said some crazy stuff that made me laugh and talk about them," I told the Holy Spirit.

Then the Holy Spirit reminded me that with the icons in the Go-Go music arena I appreciated those gifts, enjoyed those gifts from God, and prayed for those gifts whenever they had trials. All I could say was, "WOW!"

Unfortunately, we often take each other for granted. This cycle must stop. The only way it will stop is when we start seeing and caring for one another like before, especially with our families. Most people say, "Let go of the past," and you should, mainly when your past keeps you from moving into your future. I think about my past a lot, particularly with my family. Memories of our times together, the good and bad, are priceless. As I reflect, I honestly cannot believe how distant and sometimes cold we have become with one another. In the past we had much less but shared more. Now we have more and share less. I loved family gatherings. I love how we used to get a knock on the door, and it was my drunk uncle coming through just to say hi. He didn't need to call first or wait for an invitation. He came in, passed out on the couch, and stayed until he woke up. It was okay. He was safe because he was with family. I also love the memories of how the cousins loved each other and played together, but now the third and fourth generations don't know, and in some instances, don't like each other. Brothers and sisters played together in the same household. Now it saddens me that they don't talk. This must change, and the only way to make sure the necessary change happens is for everyone to stop and look in the mirror and reveal themselves to themselves. Please look in the mirror today!

The desire for material things, money, a career, and power have a stronghold on too many people, but most don't possess that same desire when it comes to protecting and looking out for family! In the end, like or not, all we have is each other...family! God commanded us to love Him with all our heart and love our neighbors as yourself. Grab hold of your family and let bygones be bygones. Forgive grievances among your family members. Be the bigger person and bring everyone together. Pray for your family and include God in your heart's desires for your family. I love my family!

In the next three chapters of this book, I shared memories and appreciation for my family. God reminded me how valuable they are and how He brought us through many hardships. In the end, the love for one another always prevailed. Don't forget to look in the mirror!

Chapter 13

MAMA, YOU KNOW I LOVE YOU!

"Honor her for all that her hands have done, and let her works bring praise at the city gate."

- Proverbs 31:31

My mama is the backbone of our family. She wanted to go to school to become a nurse. Because she had to help with her younger brothers and sisters, she didn't complete middle school. My mama ended up caring for so many others that she still fulfilled her purpose.

While growing up, I didn't understand her. I didn't realize that she was a Proverbs 31 woman. The opposite of my daddy, my mom was the disciplinarian and didn't hesitate to spank us when needed. My daddy didn't spank us. I later I learned that as a young boy, my daddy was blamed and spanked for almost everything. Many spankings were not deserved. When he was a young boy, he vowed not to spank his children. When I was young, I believed that all my mother did was go to work, come home, and spank me for something. She was strict and wouldn't let me do anything. I honestly thought I didn't' like her.

To make sure her children understood freedom and the struggle to live a better life, my mother used every opportunity to show us how to appreciate what others before us had to go through. Movie night in our house wasn't fun for me. She made us watch movies like *Roots* and *The Autobiography of Miss Jane Pittman* every year. When those movies were on the television, there were three things we couldn't do: fall asleep, laugh, or pass gas. We were only allowed to laugh at scenes in *Roots* that involved Chicken George and his hat.

Once I made a huge mistake and said, "I don't want to watch that old ugly lady no more."

I got the spanking of a lifetime.

My mother said, "You better not ever call another elderly person ugly as long as I live."

I thought she was the meanest mom on earth. During thunderstorms, in respect to the Lord, everything in the house had to be turned off and everyone had to be completely quiet. If we talked, laughed, or cried during the storms, we got it when the storm was over. I got a spanking every time there was a storm because I was scared and couldn't keep quiet, which meant I must have been bad.

During that time, I had no idea that my mama kept a lot of pain inside. Her upbringing was hard. I later found out that my daddy was abusive toward my mom before I was born. I didn't see that side of my daddy. He was handsome. A lot of women thought he was fine, and some tried to harm my mom, thinking with her out of the way they could be with my dad. Those women didn't know my mama. She would've done anything to keep her family together. During my mom's entire pregnancy with me she was sick because she was poisoned by one of those women. My mom was strong, and we both survived. The one thing my mother knew for sure is that her children were hers. She protected us at all costs. She has that same protective spirit over her grandchildren. The only difference is that now she relies on God's Word and prayer.

As a child there was no way for me to understand that my mother's plate wasn't just full, it overflowed. She tirelessly worked at being a wife and mother. My daddy was a gambler, and most of the time, he gambled and lost money needed for food and shelter. My mother worked two jobs, sometimes three, to make sure her family was fed and had a place to call home. My mama was a planner. Months before school started, she put our clothes on layaway so that each of us had at least ten new outfits for the first two weeks of school. She did the same for Christmas, shopping early and putting gifts on layaway so that I could have the joy of unwrapping dolls and toys on Christmas morning. During advertisements on television, I showed her what I wanted. I was unaware that she was paying attention and working on a plan to get those things for me. My mom was strong. She covered my daddy's shortcomings and kept the family together for as long as she could.

My family believed in Jesus. That was it! Except for funerals, I don't remember ever seeing my parents attend church, but they did watch church services on television every Sunday. My mom sent my baby brother and me to church on Sundays and Easter with the other neighborhood children during the 70's and early 80's. Every Sunday morning, my dad got dressed in his favorite suit, sat in the living room, and watched a pastor from California on the television. After watching Sunday morning service, he got the pushcart and headed for the grocery store. My daddy always cooked us a large breakfast and dinner on Sundays. My parents, whom I dearly love, did the best they could, formed from what they were taught during their upbringing and the understanding they had at the time.

I acquired my ability to clean a house and dedication to work hard from my Proverbs 31 mother. As a teenager, whenever I needed backup, I ran to my mother. I kept some things from her, but like all good mamas, she eventually found out. At the age of 16, I gave my mother a letter to let her know that I was pregnant. She immediately became more protective of me. Next, she gave my brothers and sisters some instructions.

Mom said, "I don't want no one to upset her. She needs to be happy. When you are carrying a baby, you should be clean and very happy."

I was clean for sure, but she didn't know at the time that I wasn't happy.

My mom instructed me not to watch any more of my favorite horror movies or shows with animals. She told me that everything I watched, the baby would watch, and it would affect the baby's mind. She didn't show any embarrassment about having a teenage daughter who was pregnant, nor did she hide it from anyone. My mother also embraced and brought into our family fold a young lady who was pregnant with my brother's child. At the time, my brother didn't believe the baby was his.

My mother told him, "If she says it's yours, it's yours. So, stop saying it ain't."

My mother didn't mistreat anyone. We all went to the hospital when my brother's baby was born.

"He don't look like me Ma!" my brother declared.

My mother held the baby and touched his little feet and hands, and said, "He is yours, son."

My mom told us that people always look at the face, but they need to look at other features like the hands and feet. My mom knew those little feet and hands were the image of my brother when he was born. My mom's word back then was the real DNA test.

When I went into labor, I was two blocks away from the hospital. She was eight or 10 miles away. My mother's cab driver beat the ambulance to the hospital. She and my cousin were there to greet and help me through the process. While in the elevator headed to the delivery room, my mother prayed the most impossible prayer. She prayed to the Lord with her hands in the air to let her have the baby for me. She pleaded with God and reminded Him that she already had five babies and my little body couldn't handle it. Although I was in was in a lot of pain, I laughed and so did the emergency technicians and my cousin. My mom was serious, but it let me know how much she loved me and was willing to take my pain.

Two weeks after giving birth, the paternity of my baby was questioned. My mother stood firm with me. After my daughter's support stopped, it was my mother who made sure my baby had milk, diapers, clothes, and whatever else she needed. My mom made it clear that no one was going to mistreat her firstborn grandbaby. My abuser at the time even asked for the crib back.

My mama said to him, "If you are big and bad enough, come get it. Countless times you have come into my home, and I welcomed you like family. Every day I fed you and you ate my food until you were full. I paid for that crib!" she scowled.

My mama always protected her babies. She didn't allow me to use the excuse of being a young mother to drop out school. She made sure I finished my last year of high school. She took care of my baby while preparing me to be a mother and didn't make it easy for me. She told me that a mother makes sacrifices for her children, and I needed to learn that. My mom did things like add cereal in my baby's milk after one week, even though the doctor said not to do that. She washed my baby's hair every day until that white hard crust was gone. The doctor also said not to do that.

His exact words were: "Do not touch it."

At the time, I didn't realize that my mother was protecting my daughter, even when she didn't listen the doctors. Most times, after I bathed my daughter and thought I had bathed her well, my mom smelled her. She then told me that my freshly bathed baby smelled like sour milk. She explained that I had to use my fingers like I was playing a piano to get in between the fat rolls in her neck to clean and remove the smell. I hadn't seen my mom play the piano, but that was her way of showing me how to properly wash my baby's neck.

Dressing little girls is so much fun and my baby was always stylish. When she began to walk, I wanted to buy stylish sneakers to go with her cute little outfits. My mama wasn't having none of that. She didn't allow my baby to walk in the sneakers I purchased. She insisted that she only walk in hard wood bottom baby shoes. I hated those shoes. They were ugly and outdated. When the shoes were dirty, my mom first wiped the shoes with a cloth and then polished them with white shoe polish so that my baby's hard shoes always looked new. Back then, I didn't know the purpose of the shoes, which was to help my daughter's balance and to have healthy feet. Today, my daughter still has the prettiest feet.

I had to get approval from my mom when I wanted to take my baby for visits or let her stay overnight with other family members and friends so that I could have time for myself. She had her own reasons why my baby couldn't go to certain people's houses. Once I had planned to take my daughter with me to visit a friend, but my mama wasn't having it. She said my friend's house was nasty and too many roaches were flying in the air.

"One of them roaches might get down in my grandbaby's ear. So, the answer is a big fat no!" she yelled.

That was the end of the conversation, and you know who won that fight.

My daddy had a big dog. He once told the story about when he left a big pot of pig's feet on the stove and the dog pulled the pot off the stove and ate all of it. After hearing that story, as far as my mom was concerned, his apartment was off limits too. She said that it was no way her grandbaby was ever going over there.

"That big ole dog might eat her, and besides, the people over there drink too much liquor."

My mom was right.

My baby took her first steps while we were visiting my dad's apartment. I knew it was off limits. He had a lot of company, and cups of liquor were around the coffee table. She walked around the table and sipped out of every cup on the table. Once we realized what she had done, we were horrified. That moment was the first time in my life when I saw fear in my daddy's eyes. We both knew that if my mama found out, she would kill everyone in the apartment, including me. When I returned home with my baby, I could tell she was drunk by the way she walked.

My mom kept saying, "Something is wrong with my grandbaby."

I couldn't tell my mother that her grandbaby was drunk. I didn't know what else to do. I prayed that she would calm down, but things got worse before they got better. She kept crying and profusely sweating. I was praying hard to God for Him to help my baby. She eventually fell asleep. Thank God she was okay when she woke the next morning. If I had told my mom what happened she would have gone completely insane. However, nine years later, I told her about the incident as we planned my daddy's funeral.

Although my mother and father were no longer together, they still dearly loved each other. Being apart helped them to see how much they loved each other and possibly could've worked things out. I felt there was a possibility they would reunite. I wasn't happy when my mother remarried. I was angry. I didn't want any part of the wedding planning or to be in the wedding. I did attend the wedding, but I wasn't happy. My mom didn't know why I was angry and resentful. She felt something but couldn't pinpoint the cause. Too many outside influences made it hard for my mother's marriage to work. It wasn't until she was divorced and rededicated her life to the Lord that we shared our hearts with each other about everything. My mother became at peace with letting the Lord love her!

My mother's gift from God is her ability to cook and bake. Over the years, she blessed many with her gift of cooking. When I wanted a cake, she had it ready within a few hours. She kept a supply of cake mixes as others that keep a supply of bottled water and batteries in case of an emergency. She prepares full-course meals for anyone who asks and opens her home to anyone needing a place to stay. She welcomed a lot of my daddy's siblings and their children with open arms to live with us. She raised children she didn't give birth to, but still claimed as her own. My mom treated those children like they were her own, and they received equal amounts of toys, clothes, and whatever else she provided for her own children. Now adults, they lovingly refer to her as Mama.

Before truly submitting her life to God, my mother was a fighter. I got it from her. She had no problem punching out anyone who messed with her or her children. When we were right, she protected us and when we were wrong, she quickly made us fix those wrongs. My mother is always there whenever I'm faced with hardship. Today, her load is much lighter because we both rely on the Word of God for everything in prayer. After I gave my life back to Christ and joined my church home, my mother noticed the change in my life. She saw the peace I had, and I shared with her that I rededicated my life to Christ. A few months later, my mother rededicated her life back to Christ and joined the same church home. It's now been over twenty years worshipping with my mom under the same ministry. Our relationship is even stronger and full of love and forgiveness for everyone and each other. I love you Mama!

Chapter 14

NOT WITHOUT MY DAUGHTER

"Train up a child in the way he/she should go: and when he/she is old he/she will not depart from it!"

- Proverbs 22:6

My beautiful daughter, my baby, my sweetheart, my gift from God! Let me tell you I am a proud mama! When I think of her and how proud I am that she is my daughter, there are not enough words to express how full my heart gets. I'm truly a *proud* mama! Love, prayer, forgiveness, more love, more forgiveness, more prayer, and more of everything that God has for us!

Being a teenage mother wasn't easy, nor did it come with instructions. I did the best I could with the knowledge I had at the time. One thing I knew for sure was that I didn't want to be on welfare. I wouldn't allow myself to be stuck in that system. I used to love watching the movie, *Claudine*. As a little girl I remember my mom and aunts receiving visits from the welfare people like in the movie. I didn't want that to happen to me. My mom received assistance when she moved to Washington, D.C.

back in the 70's but she was determined to come off welfare and work to provide for her family.

I was a teenage mother with a beautiful baby girl. The first week I brought her home, I didn't know what to do with my little beautiful person. All I knew was that I was responsible for her care. I called 911 two times during that first week. She spit up and kept crying. The emergency workers laughed both times. I tried to call a third time, but my mom instructed me not to pick up the phone. I called my mom while she was at work to tell her my daughter was turning pink and was trying to poop but couldn't. I was scared. My mom told me to send my brother to the store to get some corn syrup. My mom arrived home from work at her regular scheduled time. She wasn't worried because she knew what to do. My mom put a teaspoon of syrup in warm water and gave it to my baby girl. Within minutes, my baby girl had a blast, and she began to smile as my mom held her.

At that time, going to college wasn't an option. I had to get a job as soon as I finished high school so that I could provide for my child. Still dealing with a lot of trauma and pain, I wanted better for my baby girl, but I needed time to find my way and figure out how to give her a better life. I didn't always make the best decisions. I missed out on some of the most precious years with my baby girl when she was a toddler and growing into a beautiful little girl. I created memories by taking her to all the fun popular places kids enjoyed. I made sure she was dressed in the nicest clothes and had everything she needed. I thought I was doing the right thing by keeping her stylish and giving her toys. I gave her every material thing I possibly could, but we didn't have a bond with each other and that was my fault. During those years, I made sure my daughter had everything except the one and most important thing she needed most, me. As a toddler, she saw my abuser beat me several times and heard the verbal abuse I received from him and his family. I had no idea how those episodes would affect her later in life.

My daughter was in her early teens when she came to live with me fulltime again. She had no way of knowing that I was at my worst. I was fighting for my life while trying to make up for time lost with her. Now that she was living with me, and we were spending more time together, I began to fear that she would become me. I didn't want my daughter to experience what I had lived through and was still going through. I did my best to protect her from it. She didn't know that I was trying my best to cover her. During the time, I was doing life my way without God. I messed up bad.

I didn't know how to explain to my daughter how much I loved her with words. I did my best to show her by my actions. I was working two jobs. I often called home from my night job to talk to her about her day at school. One night, as we were talking about her day, she told me about an incident with a boy in the neighborhood. He slapped her in her face. On my drive home, I relived the abuse in my life—the slaps, the kicks, the punches. I wasn't going to allow my daughter to live with abuse as I had. I needed to end it before it got started. I didn't want her to grow up thinking it was okay for a man or boy to hit her. During the drive home, I made up my mind that we were going to the boy's house to speak with him and his parents. The time didn't matter to me. As soon as I got home, I scooped her up and headed to the boy's house. I spoke with his mother and told her what happened. I then harshly spoke to him and told him that he better not put his hands on her ever again. Before leaving, I made my daughter slap him in the face in front of his mother. I made her slap him again because I felt she didn't slap him hard enough the first time. Days after the incident with the boy, a girl started a fight with my daughter. Again, although it was late when I got home, I went to the girl's house to speak with her mom. The mom and I spoke in detail about what happened between the girls. She scolded her daughter and then apologized. We became good neighbors and made sure our girls became friends.

I was overprotective of my daughter. The thought of anyone hitting her sent me over the edge. She used to love riding her bike on weekends. One Saturday I noticed that she wasn't going outside to ride her bike. I asked why she wasn't riding her bike. She hesitated and then told me she was being bullied. I was enraged! I found out who the bullies were and went straight to their home to speak to their mother, who by the way was ghetto as hell. Little did she know, I could get ghetto too. Trying to work things out with a ghetto parent only created more frustration which I didn't need. I called the police to report the incident so that they could have it on file. On Monday morning, I was at the school to speak with the principle about the bullies. My daughter was afraid. Every morning and evening I waited outside for her to make sure they didn't hurt her. She felt embarrassed but I didn't care. I wanted to make sure she was safe. My co-workers laughed at me because I used a week of my vacation leave to stay home with my daughter until I felt she was safe from the neighborhood bullies.

I was traumatized all over again because my daughter was upset. I had been there before and understood the emotional turmoil. My next step was to whip their butt myself and then deal with the consequences. Fortunately, it didn't happen. I took the appropriate steps, and the matter was eventually resolved. Upon returning to work, my supervisor advised not to take off work again for little incidents like that because children were going to get into fights. My manager didn't know anything about my life and my trauma, nor the fact that it wasn't just an incident when children were fighting. She was being bullied.

However, I firmly told her, "You have four little bears. I have one bear. Therefore, your four little bears have each other as support and back up when needed. My little bear only has me, and I am always going to be there."

Out of fear, I smothered my daughter. She didn't have any freedom, and I was always on edge with worry about her when she out of my sight. When she wasn't with me, the only time I felt relieved was when I knew she was with my family, my husband, and our church members. I knew I was smothering her, but I was coming from a good place. I was only trying to protect her. Eventually, she began to resent me because of it. Our relationship became hard and painful. I no longer recognized her. She turned into a rebellious teenager who hated her mother. Dealing with an insubordinate teenager was hard, but it is worse because I was depressed and still dealing with my own trauma and having a hard time keeping it together. I didn't know what to do. I was under so much stress. I began to hear voices in my head and couldn't stop it. They began to control me. I once spanked my daughter with a tremendous amount of force because of the many voices in my head. My daughter was unaware that I was going through anything, let alone the severity of it. She simply thought that I was a mean out of control overprotective mom.

I was still getting use to my new life with Christ and had no clue about the correct way to pray the Word of God concerning my daughter and our situation. I met with my first lady, and she shared a book with me called *Prayers That Avail Much* by Germaine Copeland. She told me to pray the prayer for a teenager. Before I read it, I just knew my rebellious teenager would be addressed, but to my surprise it was the total opposite. As I began to read and pray, I realized that I was the problem. One of the Scriptures in the prayer reminded parents not to provoke children to anger. Colossians 3:21 stated, "Parents, provoke not your children to anger, lest they be discouraged." A light bulb came on. I began to repent and ask God to forgive me for the hurtful things I spoke over and to my child. Out of fear, I attacked her physically and verbally, trying to get her to live right.

God knew I needed help with my daughter. I began to bring her to church with me. God had some amazing people in our church to help us. Ministers in the youth department were assigned to her, and they took her and the other children under their care. Even though my daughter wasn't happy with some of the ministers, she respected and honored them. I was able to relax and breathe; no longer feeling as though I had to do everything on my own. My daughter now had godly influences in her life to help her. I appreciate everyone that has sown their time, prayers, and love into her. It truly takes a village to raise a child.

I found out that God so love us! John 3:16 says, "God so loved the world, that he gave his only begotten son, that whosoever believeth in him should not perish, but have everlasting life." *God so loved us.* For many, many, years, I thought His love was based upon my actions. I felt worthless as a woman, mother, wife, friend, daughter, sister, auntie, etc. My revelation and understanding came when I was hit with a devastating life changing blow. My baby, my only child, my beautiful daughter told me she was gay. I was shocked, heartbroken, and in disbelief. Naturally, I expected to one day to have a son-in-law and beautiful grandchildren. I had plans to love and spoil rotten my grandchildren. I also felt like I could make up for some of the time I lost with my daughter through my grandchildren. All sort of things began to run through my mind, and I blamed myself. I tried to think of how it must have started. Maybe it was because she saw me constantly abused when she was a toddler. I blamed myself for allowing her to repeatedly watch the movie *The Color Purple* when she was a child. She watched the movie so many times that she was able to quote scenes. One day, while playing in her large playhouse, she began to imitate the character Celie.

"Suge coming! Suge coming!" she said as she pretended to act like Celie.

She was a little girl, and it was funny. I just didn't know how or what happened. But I loved her even more than before if this is possible. I wasn't going to reject and lose my daughter again. I know many people that have gay children. I witnessed how ashamed some of them were and how embarrassed they felt when their children came out. It was harder for some because they were Christians. I didn't want to be that person, but I was for a minute. I realized we all made the same mistake—we made it about us and not our children. We cared too much what others thought and rejected our children. I knew I had to get past how I felt and what I wanted for myself because it wasn't about me. I was self-absorbed and I didn't think about what my daughter was going through.

My daughter sat me down and opened her heart and told me where it began. I felt like a nuclear bomb went off inside me! I wanted to get to the root of it. A neighbor's daughter fondled her when she was a toddler. Later, the little girl my daughter fell in love with was someone I knew. It began when they were in elementary school. She grew out of it, had relationships with men, and had children of her own. As my daughter shared details with me, I was horrified, angry, and hurt. I wanted to confront the young lady's mother and grandmother because they were like family to me, but I didn't.

God began to show me that He knows our end from the beginning and nothing in the middle was a surprise to Him. In the natural, I couldn't go after anyone. I had to get my heart right, repent, and go into prayer. I told God that I didn't know what to do. To this day, I only have two answers: love and acceptance. One night I uncontrollably cried—hard. I couldn't stop my tears. As I begged God to make it go away, the Holy Spirit told me to just love her.

"Lord, I do. This is why I'm crying out to you."

The Lord said, "So love her! She is still your gift from me. She is still your child, and no matter what, this will never change. Sherry! Despite of your flaws, mistakes, shortcomings, and sins, I still love you."

My heart dropped, "I get it Lord!"

That's her testimony and no matter what, He created her and knows the plans He has for her.

God took me down memory lane. He reminded me of the people that are dear to my heart who were gay. I unconditionally loved them, and they knew I dearly loved them.

God said, "What about your childhood friends? What about your high school bestie? What about the attorneys? What about all your little cousins and one of your favorite nephews? What about the television show host?"

God showed me that when I see these individuals, I light up like a Christmas tree, full of love and acceptance, and they know without a shadow of doubt that I love them.

"You love them like I love you. Do the same with your daughter because I know you love her too."

God reminded me of His love for the world. John 3:16 (NKJV) states, "For God so loved the world that He gave His only begotten Son, that whoever believes in Him should not perish but have everlasting life." I made a heartfelt decision that no matter what it took, I was going to believe the report of the Lord! I wasn't going to waste precious days and years worried about my daughter's sexuality. I wanted to love her each second of the day for the rest of my life. I was devastated when I learned how she was introduced to lesbianism. I thought it was either my fault or a generational curse.

It's no such thing as a generational curse since Jesus paid the price on Calvary. He became sin for our sins. He became sin for everyone, even those that don't believe. 2 Corinthians 5:21 declared, "God made Him who had no sin to be sin for us, so that in him we might become the righteousness of God." Who does this include? I believe everyone—you, me, gay, Americans, Europeans, Spanish, Asian, Jewish, and so on—everyone on the face of this earth. Now, there are generational behaviors that can run in a family.

For those who are believers in Christ, Jesus last words on the cross were, "It is finished."

When something is finished, it is over and done. In the natural you can finish something and then go back and add, revise, redo, or even upgrade, but one that cannot be revised is Jesus. Mankind loves to express what is and what's not acceptable to God. I asked the Holy Spirit why mankind has a need to always have an opinion and to be right about everything. The Holy Spirit told me to read Genesis 1:25-31 (NIV):

"But this time read with understanding. And God said, Let us make man in our image, after our likeness: and let them have dominion over the fish of the sea, and over the fowl of the air, and over the cattle, and over all the earth, and over every creeping thing that creepeth upon the earth. So God created man in his own image, in the image of God created he him; male and female created he them. And God blessed them, and God said unto them, be fruitful, and multiply, and replenish the earth, and subdue it: and have dominion over the fish of the sea, and over the fowl of the air, and over every living thing that moveth upon the earth. And God said, Behold, I have given you every herb bearing seed, which is upon the face of all the earth, and every tree, in the which is the fruit of a tree yielding seed; to you it shall be for meat. And to every beast of the earth, and to every fowl of the air, and to everything that creepeth upon the earth, wherein there is life, I have given every green herb for meat: and it was so. And God saw everything that he had made, and, behold, it was very good. And the evening and the morning were the sixth day."

With this understanding, I see mankind was given authority, but none of that authority was given over each other. Male and female were created equal. The fall of Adam and Eve caused mankind to live under the law. Mankind was unable to keep the laws of God, therefore God gave us Jesus. The sacrifice of Jesus is eternal life, grace, and mercy to mankind. We are all under His grace. Jesus put mankind back in the right standing with God's plan from the beginning. The world looks at Christians through a microscope because we constantly profess that when you come to Jesus to come as you are, and that Jesus loves you and died for you. We confess that everyone is welcome in the beloved, but then we put one Christian or a group of people such as the gay community under the law and sadly not grace.

I had another conversation with Holy Spirit about love, kindness, and acceptance. I'm sharing my heart between the gay people and the Christians I know. I've had encountered one hateful gay person in my life, a former co-worker. Before I knew how hateful and mean-spirited that person was, another co-worker experienced it before me. I saw my co-worker in tears, silently sobbing at her desk to the point that her blouse was wet from tears. She didn't share her reason with me or other co-workers nor file a complaint. She eventually resigned. I became the next victim of the mean-spirited person. I was still dealing with other trauma in my life while trying to provide for my daughter. The co-worker added another form of torture. The co-worker used their position and authority over me to torture me. The co-worker made sure there were no witnesses to the bad behavior and outrage. I went to human resources to talk about what was happening to me, but without witnesses, there wasn't a thing they could do. To top things off, the co-worker spoke highly of me to others and acted like I was the best employee and doing a great job. The co-worker cried in the meetings with human resources, but once alone with me, the vicious cycle continued.

I had too much going on in my personal life. The stress and mistreatment at work caused me to have my second mental breakdown. Many in authority at the workplace used their position to harass people under them. I was diagnosed with depression, which was major, and spent three months in therapy. I returned to work and that co-worker immediately started the same behavior. It went on every day during my first week back at work. I prayed and cried out to God in the bathroom stall, asking Him to please open another door for me in the workplace. When I returned to my desk, I received a call from a previous manager that had an opening at a new workplace. My earnest heartfelt prayer was answered. Every other gay person I have encountered had the fruit of spirit described in Galatians 5:22-23 (KJV): "But the fruit of the Spirit is love, joy, peace, longsuffering, gentleness, goodness, faith, meekness, temperance: against such there is no law." I had to remove my judgmental mindset that stemmed from *religion* and receive the heart of agape love that Jesus has for us.

I began to share with the Holy Spirit that I encountered hundreds of hateful and mean-spirited Christians. I know because I used to be one in the beginning of my walk with God, full of rules and regulations. I still wanted to curse people out, fight, and hold grudges. I was unforgiving, stubborn, and so many other things. The body of Christ doesn't have the authority or light we should have in the world because we are so divided, and we aren't loving each other with the same love Jesus has for everyone. Love must be at the forefront in everything we say and do. No one should ever feel any type of ill feeling whenever they enter a place a worship or encounter a Christian. When we are in God's place of worship, we shouldn't overlook people, roll our eyes at others, or exclude anyone.

When my daughter comes home, she dreads going to her childhood church. She hasn't felt rejection from our pastors, but some people walked past her and gave a mean look. I consistently remind her that she belongs to God, just like they do, and to walk through the doors into God's house with her head held high!

"God will deal with those who reject you. Keep your heart right baby."

I will always encourage my daughter and anyone else who feels rejected and unloved.

Everything we go through we will go through it together because love is better than rejection. I had to give my anxiety about this chapter in our lives to God, for He cares for us. This is not easy. I love my daughter and I trust God with her life. When I stand on judgement day and the books are opened, I don't want to be called out for not loving my daughter or anyone else. When we stand before Almighty God, we all will give an account for everything done on earth. When you stand, you will stand alone; not for someone else but for yourself and give an account for every unrepented thing. I want to love like my God, love like my Jesus, and love like I want love and acceptance.

I don't condone my daughter's lifestyle, but I have accepted it. I had to stop trying to be God and release my cares about her life once and for all to God. I had to release my fears and anxiety once and for all to God and go on with my life. My daughter choices are her choices, just like mine are mine. The Bible clearly says in Proverbs 22:6 (NKJV), "Train up a child in the way he should go: and when he is old, he will not depart from it." I totally stand on two Scriptures concerning my children: "But the seed of the righteous shall be delivered," (Proverbs 11:21b) and "Lo children are a heritage of the Lord: and the fruit of the womb is his reward!" (Psalms 127:3). I have shared with my daughter to keep the Lord first in her life and to know His voice.

I know what my daughter has been through and no mother who has a relationship with the Lord wants their children to intentionally hurt or be harmed. I am protective of my daughter, and everyone else I care about. My flesh can go from zero to a 100 in a second without thinking. God is still working in me. It's good to know that my helper, the Holy Spirit, dwells on the inside and knows how to handle my flesh!

Do I pray for the company my daughter keeps? Most definitely. I've witnessed people pretend to be who they aren't. They look for others to take care of them. These people are predators and simply looking to take advantage of someone. They haven't worked a day in their life and want to reap the benefits and eat the fruit from the hard labor of others. No one wants this for their child, no matter how old they get. God has given me wisdom and discernment concerning my daughter. I know my daughter is an adult, but she is still my gift from God! I stay in constant prayer and intercession for her. More than anything, we love each other, and we love through everything we go through together. I'm blessed, and I thank God that He helped us through many difficult times and will continue as long as we keep Him first.

Many have rejected my daughter because of the way she looks, her sexual preference, or just in general. God loves her. We love her, including, me, her two dads, her grandmother, her aunts and uncles, her friends, family, my friends, our pastors, and our puppies Bella and Precious. Love outweighs hate! Dominique Demetris Walker I salute you! I'm proud to be called your mama! You are a smart, intelligent, humble, and a caring woman of God! I love how you sought to understand and have a relationship with your biological father and love him with all your heart. You chose to love us, honor us, and accept the good and the bad in us. I love how you honor your stepdad. You've shown my husband respect and love. You took the pieces of the past and made them your steppingstones to unconditionally love everyone. I'm proud of you, for you have worked hard at being a good person to society, the United States Armed Forces, your family, and friends. You could only do this by the love of God for others that dwells in your heart.

I thank God for another chance and a restored relationship with my daughter. She has become, and most likely always was, the most loving, caring, beautiful woman of God! I had been blinded by the devil and couldn't see who she truly is. Her kindness, generosity, love for family and everyone is amazing! To know her is to love and appreciate the gift she is. The devil tried his best to kill my precious gift, but God! I know your latter will be greater than your former! Ephesians 6:2-3 (NKJV) states, "'Honor your father and mother,' which is the first commandment with promise: 'that it may be well with you and you may live long on the earth.'" I love you daughter!

Chapter 15

MY TWO HEARTBEATS: MY SISTERS

Always be humble and gentle. Be patient with each other, making allowance for each other's faults because of your love.

- Ephesians 4:2 (NLT)

My two sisters! Three sisters who were born in the month of August on the 11th, 23rd, and 31st. What a supernatural blessing! Three sisters who couldn't wear each other shoes: 10.0, 11.0, and 12.0. Three sisters who couldn't wear each other clothes: small, tall, and plus. Three sisters who had one thing in common: each other!

I haven't expressed to my two older sisters how much they mean to me. I think it's because I overstepped my boundaries by thinking I was in charge. I was the most stubborn little sister on earth. I didn't like them telling me what to do. I knew I was stuck with them. No matter what, they will always be in my life. I had many reasons to be mad at them while growing up. Vanessa helped me to write my name when I was in kindergarten. She is the one who changed my name from Sherry to Sherrie. She showed me how to write my name that way. I did and accepted the name change from her. Sherry is on my birth certificate, and after 45 years, I must use it. One day, Vanessa was braiding my hair. I asked her not to use the cigarette lighter to burn the ends of my braids. She knew I had a Jeri curl underneath. She did and up in flames my hair went. I was so mad! She wasn't allowed to do my hair again. I was mad at Carolyn because she made me wash the dishes all the time. I explained to her several times that I was only washing my plate, my fork, and my cup! She still made me do it. My big sisters used their authority to max back then.

After years past and I was in my thirties, God began dealing with me about my heart toward my sisters. I felt abandoned by them during my teen years. Correction was needed in my heart concerning them. My oldest sister Carolyn was like my second mom. She took care of her four siblings while our parents worked two and sometimes three jobs. She cooked dinner, bathed us, helped with homework, ironed our school clothes, and did hers too. To keep order in the home, those were her duties. She had the authority to spank everyone, and she spanked me the most. Carolyn didn't get to enjoy her teenage years. She couldn't go to after school events or have fun with friends because she had to take care of her siblings. She missed out on so much. When she was old enough to breakout, she took off. I was happy but then I became sad because I missed her a lot. I felt like a piece of me was missing. I believed that if she was with me, I wouldn't have had the trauma in my life. She was my bold and beautiful protector who went away to start her life called freedom. When my daughter was born, she was excited but forgot I was a teen mom. She took my baby to church for her first Easter. When she returned my baby home, her dress was ripped, barrettes and ribbons were missing, and she was uncontrollably crying.

"What happened?" I asked.

"Your baby cried the whole time. Here, take her! Your baby tore her dress and ripped out the barrettes."

Carolyn came over every week to see her niece and brought her the biggest chocolate chip cookie ever. She watched her eat that cookie to pieces while messing up her clothes and hair. When Carolyn left, I had a big mess to clean up. She offered several times to babysit but little Dominique wasn't having it. Now, you can't keep themselves apart. I love how my daughter honors her aunts with respect.

My middle sister Vanessa, my superstar, a gorgeous tall, beautiful woman, made a statement everywhere she went. I thought she would be the next big thing in

America. My name changed to Vanessa's Baby Sister! People I didn't know called me that, and it felt so good. When someone calls me that today, I am reminded about how precious my sister is to me. She was especially protective and watchful over me. During my teen years, my sister was dealing with drug abuse. She was no longer able to protect me, and I was hurt. Vanessa went away for a few years, came back, and had to go back for few more years. She had many challenges. God had her on His mind. It was a beautiful thing to see. God has blessed her with a wonderful husband who adores and loves her through everything. My brother-in-law Anthony is the best. He was tailored just for my sister Vanessa. It was such a blessing to be allowed to plan their wedding. They have two sons who loves and cares for them. Her sons honored our daddy by giving her away together to her husband. Our daddy would have approved my brother-in-law Anthony 100%.

My first lady held a Women Walking in Word (WWW) meeting one Saturday. That meeting was about sisters. Dr. Dee had all her sisters on the panel. She asked selected members of the church to pair with their sisters and dance. I knew the meeting was about sisters, but I didn't think to invite them. The meeting was heartfelt. I was without my sisters. It hit me like a ton of bricks when I realized it. So much was going in my life and in theirs too. I didn't know how I was going to reconnect with them. I was ashamed to let them get close to me. I had hope through the Word of God! Today, I love my sisters and I'm thankful we are together, reaching out to each other, helping each other, praying for one another, getting on each other nerves again, but more than anything, loving the Lord together! Love and acceptance are most important. Carolyn, you are still my bold and beautiful! Vanessa, you are still my superstar! I am my sister's keeper!

Along with my two heartbeats, I have two brothers who I love dearly. The eldest brother Carroll, Jr. is a gentle giant, a quiet and peaceful man, better known as Dohickey. He didn't interact much, but his love showed through his actions. He is always willing to lend a helping hand. Carroll didn't get into trouble. He was the one who had to get the switches for my mom to spank us when she got off work. Some days he picked switches with thorns on them. I threw those switches out the window. He picked the ones that looked like ropes that could be wrapped around us during the spanking. I threw those out the window too. We had to train him how to get the ones that were dark brown. Those broke in half, and they didn't hurt as bad. He came back with 50 switches. By the time my mom got home, she only had about 10 switches to spank us because I threw them out the window. My brother Carroll was the one who God had in place to save my life. He walked in my house the day I tried to commit suicide. Carroll found me and called for help, thereby preserving my life. I thank God that my life didn't end 34 years ago. My brother Carroll is a wonderful husband and father. Now he is the life of our family gatherings. Still quiet but loves our family gatherings. He loves creating memories by taking pictures and recording events. God has blessed him with a wonderful wife and daughter who loves everything about my brother.

My baby brother Marcel and I are only one year apart. We were at odds growing up, but no one could mess with him. When I found out about it, I whipped plenty of children's butts, male and female, for messing with my baby brother. He didn't want my help, but my big sister power kicked in. For many years, the devil tried hard to cause division between me and my baby brother. I constantly prayed for him and for me to keep my heart right. I continued to keep in mind that he was my brother and all he had done for me over the years. My brother Marcel did his best to help me through my hard teenage years. He was smaller than my abuser and did his best to protect me when he found out. When I was pregnant with my daughter, I had cravings for fast-food fish sandwiches. Marcel walked two and three times a day for 10 blocks to get me what I wanted. One day, he walked with two dollars' worth of pennies to get me a fish sandwich. He was mad, but he went. I don't know what he did to that sandwich on the way back, but I ate it. I thank God for my baby brother. He is a wonderful husband and father to his children. I love you my baby brother.

I'm very grateful to God. He has blessed me with some amazing in-laws. I love how each of them love my siblings with all their hearts. May God continue to bless each life, each union, and their children.

Chapter 16

MY VARSITY CHEERLEADERS

"Iron sharpen iron; so a man sharpen the countenance of his friend."

- Proverbs 27:17

Cheerleaders are the best! Back in high school, I tried out for the varsity team. Over a hundred girls tried out. While going to the gym door, a boy from my neighborhood said to me that I wasn't going to make the team. He looked at my outer appearance. I was skinny, had a Jheri curl, and my hair was cut close that I looked like a boy wearing a skirt. Regardless of what he said about my appearance, I knew I could cheer and was going to make the team. I had the confidence because I practiced ahead of time. I did a split in one day by stretching between two chairs in my dining room on and off throughout the day. The day the announcement was made over the loudspeaker at school. My name was broadcast next to the end. I was excited. Only 15 of us made the team that year. We had to learn the cheers, and for some, it was hard to catch on. As a team, we worked together to make sure they learned. No one was cut from our team, but some did leave on their own. Cheerleaders are special and they cheer the team to victory. After a loss, the cheerleaders still cheer for the team as they head back home. When it was a home game, the cheerleaders pumped up the fans in the stands!

Since my walk with Christ, I have gained many cheerleaders and fans over time. I appreciate each one. I have a varsity team that has been with me from the day they made my team. They haven't stopped cheering for me. They proudly wear the uniform of friendship! My varsity cheerleaders are the best! They pray, listen, tell me the truth, cry, adjust, cover me, share their time, and encourage me. I haven't had to doubt their friendship and love towards me. With my craziness, mood swings, and sometimes isolating myself, they haven't changed towards me. I love them. They come in different shapes, but their insides are the same. They love me!

The Bible tells us that a friend will lay down his life for his friends. I have a lot of friends and it's hard to name them all. I have a few that have been with me throughout my journey, from childhood playing in the dirt, school mates, coworkers who have become friends, and some who were strategically sent to me by God!

Let's Meet My Squad

My Kim is the jelly on my peanut butter sandwich. We have been friends seen 1979. Kim is a friend who taught me how to stand up for myself when I was little girl. I was being bullied by many in our neighborhood. One day she made me fight back and made sure it was a fair fight. I won that fight! Kim shared everything with me, even her mom, who became my second mom. Our brothers got into a little fight, to the point when our dads had harsh words. Kim and I weren't going to let our brothers ruin our friendship. We were the glue to mend our dads together, and they became the best of friends. We were two mischievous little girls, always on the scene whenever stuff was going on in the neighborhood. At the age of 12, we had a hookup at the liquor store. We often went through the woods and sat on Fred's porch to drink our bumper bull beers. That ended quickly. One day, as I was drinking a beer, I thought I heard Fredrick Douglas' voice telling me to get off his porch. Now he has been dead since 1895. I didn't drink beer again. Kim was the one who told the lie to my husband that I liked him back in 1990. She knows who I was then and who I am in Christ today.

During one of my darkest times in my life, Kim was not around. She was incarcerated. It was her first offense, and the judge threw the book at her. I didn't go to see her because every year she told me she was coming home. For seven long years, I believed her. Before she came home, I was hanging out at clubs, fighting, and I lost my dad. Life was hard without my friend. Years went by and still no Kim. When I dedicated my life to Christ, I added her on my prayer list every day. I began to send Kim tapes of our Sunday services. She gave her life to Christ and consistently prayed for me. She made a promise that when she was released, she would join the same church home with me. God expedited blessings in her life. She immediately got a great job, had her own apartment, and was reunited with her mom. I had my friend back in my life and we both are growing together in Christ!

My Stacey is the captain of my squad. She is also a childhood friend since 1979. She endured so much in her life. She lost her first love to gun violence. I was trying to be by her side and cheer her up. I couldn't stop my tears. I loved her husband, and to lose him that way was awful.

As she was cracking up laughing at me, she said, "Sherrie, you supposed be cheering me up. Get yourself together."

When I had a crazy idea or vision, she encouraged me to go for it. She supports me and has tremendously sown into my life. She isn't negative. Sometimes during my lowest points, she was the one to remind me about how far I've come and pushed me to keep going. The thing that I love about her the most is that she always gives me something to laugh about, no matter how bad thing are. Whenever I came around the way or visit, the first thing I get is her beautiful smile and her hilarious laugh afterwards. We laughed the first minute before saying a word. It's always a joy to be around her. Ever when she is mad while expressing herself, she is laughing. When she walked into the funeral home at my father's wake. We instantly began to laugh, even with tears in my eyes. My friend's presence brought me joy. We laughed our way through so many hardships. Stacey touched my heart the day she was baptized. I was there to witness the wonderful occasion and to celebrate her, but she told me that I inspired her. She also told me that by rededicating her life back to Christ, she truly understood my forgiving heart towards others. I love that she is a risk-taker, but she better not get back on another hot air balloon! I love my Stacey.

My Sonia is the kindest friend one could have. I had her shoulder to cry on when I was being beaten. She wiped my tears away. She drove me around in her mother's station wagon for hours in the middle of the night until I got sleepy. During those drives, she just let me cry my heart out. We both had buckets of tears flowing. She was there to listen, never judged me, and prayed that one day, that part of my life would soon be over. She covered up a lot of my bald spots in my hair. One day she did my hair. I got a fresh haircut and perm. I felt so pretty. Within one hour after getting home, a bucket of water was thrown on my hair by my abuser. Every time my hairstyle was destroyed, she used her time and talent to restore it. She didn't reject her broken friend. I love you, my Sonia.

My Fremanda is a rare diamond, a color that I haven't seen. My Fremanda was sent to me by God, tailor-made just for me. What I love and appreciate about her the most is how she loves God with all her heart. She goes to war in prayer for others. I love how she loves her birth sisters and one brother. She covers them in her heart and in prayers. She is beautiful, but her inner beauty is radiant! We worked at the same company, but only greeted each other. We lived in the same neighborhood in two places, but we didn't connect until I joined the Spirit of Faith Christian Center. She was a member when the church first started at Anacostia High School. My Fremanda took me under her wings at church. She shared the Word of God with me, helped me through some of the most hurtful episodes at church, and told me not to give up. She constantly prays for me and my family. She taught me through her life how to honor and pray for our pastors. She is proud to be my friend, and it shows. She doesn't care if I sometimes dress in rainbow-bright colors, and it appears to be a black and white party. She knows I'm special! Most people are shocked to know that she is my friend and loves me. I love you My Fremanda!

My Tia, my beloved Tia! Where do I began? She was a coworker and now is my sister-for-life! Encourage, encouraging, encouragement is written in her heart! My Tia was my workplace angel for many years. She believed in me. Tia stayed after work for four to five hours to help get me prepared for assignments that I was unsure about how to complete. I continued to change my mind at least 800 times about taking the plunge for a promotion by going to another city to work in our new office. My Tia took the "en" from the word "encourage" and changed it to courage! While she was Dorothy, I felt like the lion! She made sure I made it to see the wizard! My Tia always became upset for me whenever I was mistreated by other coworkers that turned on me. When I was hurt, she was hurt.

My Tia told me, "When God shakes our tree to rid it from the bad fruit in our lives, stop picking it up! That bad fruit is on the ground for a reason. We need to stop picking it up and shining it off and putting it back in our aprons to hold on to! It is on the ground in the first place for a reason. The connection doesn't have to continue in our lives. The shiniest and best-looking fruit appears to be good, but it is rotten to the core!"

God can see it. We can't see into someone's heart like He can. In a nutshell: stop giving a pass and allow someone to hurt you, including the ones in the workplace. Be kind and nice but do your work and go home to your family. My Tia has inspired me.

"Sherrie, you must trust that things will always workout," she reassured.

I first met Tia in the workplace, and she quickly became a wonderful friend. She uplifts and prays for me. When I fell back into depression, she was there, reminding me about how God gives me the victory in every situation. Tia was there when I was financially at my lowest. We have seen each other through rough patches including a scarcity of salary without question until we were able to see the light at the end of the tunnel. I love you, My Tia!

My little big brother Von went from co-worker to brother. 2 Corinthians 6:6 (NLT) declares, "We prove ourselves by our purity, our understanding, our patience, our kindness, by the Holy Spirit within us, and by our sincere love." My brother V lived the above Scripture concerning me. I entered, more like interrupted, his life in

July of 2000. I'm not leaving. A typical day in office after my duties were done included having a cup of coffee on my desk and my office door ajar just to hear my brother V come in without taking off his coat.

"Shut up Sherrie!" he shouted.

That was his way of saying good morning to me! He had the messiest office ever. I got tired of seeing it. I often went in there and cleaned it up. Then, brother V couldn't find anything he was working on. He taught me a valuable lesson.

He said, "What appears to be a mess in someone else life could just be a blessing in disguise."

It's the same way in life. Some things may look like a mess and out of order, but in the end, it will come together. We encouraged each other while in the office. No matter what went down, we knew we were together and ready to face the outcome. When I met him, he was making homemade soap while working full-time. From time to time, he brought in a new bar of soap for me to try. I think he was experimenting on me. The products were good. It was a blessing to see that no matter what life brought, God completes the gift you have in you. My Brother V reminded me to not give up on my dreams. He, along with his children, are living out a dream that he and his late wife LaShawn Lindsey envisioned over 25 years ago. We are blessed to be a blessing! Thank you for having my back through some of the most difficult times in the workplace and in my life. I love my Von "Soapman" Lindsey!

Chapter 17

MY HELPER

But the Comforter, which is the Holy Ghost, whom the
father will send in my name, he shall teach you all
things, and bring all things to your remembrance,
whatsoever I have said to you.

- John 14:26

The day I began to pray in the Holy Ghost with the evidence of speaking in tongues was a day I didn't want to attend church. It was youth Sunday when the children were going to sing and have fun. The Holy Spirit instructed me to go to church anyway, and I went. During the praise and worship portion of service I closed my eyes and began to receive the words in my heart from the soloist. The words were bow down and worship Him. I began to bow down, and I went into another place in my heart. When I came up, I was praying in my heavenly language. Acts 2:4 (KJV) states, "And they were all filled with the Holy Ghost and began to speak with other tongues as the Spirit gave them utterance." I gained the power I needed in prayer to break some strongholds off my life and family. I began to clearly hear God's voice. Even though I was still dealing with a torture mind, the

Holy Spirit was speaking over the condemning voices in my head. I had so many voices in my head. The only thing I could do to shut those voices up were to eat some pineapple Now and Later candy. Those voices loved that pineapple candy. One time while in church, to keep the voices quite I ate about ten packs of those candies before service ended. Another time during service, those voices began to pulse in my head, so much so that it gave me a headache. In my mind, the voices were arguing, then they began to fight. It was like they were throwing chairs at each other, flat out fighting. The argument was about what ministry of helps to serve in at church. One voice wanted to play the drums, another voice wanted to dance, the other voice wanted to be in a girl's group, and the last one wanted to sing. The voices began to tell each other they can't do any of those things. I heard a louder voice telling them to shut up. That voice was the Holy Spirit, and they did. The Holy Spirit stated that it was a stronghold to be seen, a show-off spirit. I couldn't do any of those things, but I had a need to be seen. Not only did the Holy Spirit quiet those voices, but He didn't want me to use candy to satisfy those strongholds. It may sound crazy but it's true. The Bible made clear what was happening. "The weapons we fight with are not the weapons of the world. On the contrary, they have divine power to demolish strongholds. We demolish arguments and every pretension that sets itself up against the knowledge of God, and we take captive every thought to make it obedient to Christ. And we will be ready to punish every act of disobedience, once your obedience is complete," states 2 Corinthians 10:4-6 (NIV). According to Philippians 2:5-8 (NIV), "Not looking to your own interests but each of you to the interests of the others. In your relationships with one another, have the same mindset as Christ Jesus: Who, being in very nature God, didn't consider equality with God something to be used to his own advantage; rather, he made himself nothing by taking the very nature of a servant, being made in human likeness. And being found in appearance as a man, he humbled himself." God knew I truly wanted to serve others, and over time the Holy Spirit directed me to serve in an area that was dear to my heart. I sowed my time where I needed help in my life. I needed help with my daughter, so I began to service in the youth department for several years. Once I left the youth department, I began serving in our women's ministry. I wanted better for all women. Serving in the women's ministry helped me to understand how valuable I was to God.

In 1997 I experienced a trying time. I opened my apartment up to a family for a place to stay during a hard time. Within less than 24 hours, my place was destroyed. Everything I work for was ruined. I made a vow that the next time I saw the individual, I was going to whip that person's butt. I made that promise over my father's grave. At that time the person's possessions were still in my apartment. A few of my friends told me to destroy the items. One woman of God constantly prayed with me at work and told me to release the items. I was hurt and always crying. I eventually released the items without destroying anything. Fast forward to the year 2001. I finally ran into the individual. I had a change of heart due to the Holy Spirit and the love of Christ in me.

The Holy Spirit corrected me and said, "If you were in that person's shoes, you would have done the same thing, but probably worse."

The individual didn't look well, seemed extremely ill. Later that evening, I began to pray heartfelt prayers. I reached out to others that cared about that individual. The Holy Spirit shared with me how I was to handle that hurtful chapter in my life and led me to Matthew 5:6-9 (KJV), which stated, "Blessed are they which do hunger and thirst after righteousness: for they shall be filled. Blessed are the merciful: for they shall obtain mercy. Blessed are the pure in heart: for they shall see God. Blessed are the peacemakers: for they shall be called the children of God," and Matthew 5:44 (KJV), "But I say unto you, love your enemies, bless them that curse you, do good to them that hate you, and pray for them which despitefully use you, and persecute you." I knew to do the right thing and turn the other cheek. In 1998, God had already blessed me with my first house and completely restored my possession. I have no regrets, even though I didn't receive an apology.

The devil challenged me when I heard God tell me to speak in church, especially to my pastor. Of the twenty years of being a partner in my church home, I've only shared with my pastor two times in front of the whole congregation what Holy Spirit told me to say. Scared and terrified, I obeyed and said what God laid on my heart. During one Bible study, my pastor shared that He was invited to a meeting with the president of the United States. The first time he met with the president, backlash from all directions was targeted at him. To go a second time might have been out of the question. I was attacked at work for being a member of my church. The Holy Spirit told me to go up to the front and speak what He laid on my heart to say to my pastor. I reminded my pastor that he asked God to send to him the world's rejects and that's what made me join the ministry.

"I felt your heart at that moment. It looks like our president is the world's most rejected person right now."

Some of the pastoral staff agreed with me and said to my pastor that it was what he asked God to do. It was hilarious, and he was touched. We laughed. God already knew that my pastor was going again. My confidence level grew. I knew I heard from God to say it. I'm not a member that's in my pastor's face. I'm better at praying for them.

One Sunday while at church, the Holy Spirit had to abruptly cast down a thought the devil threw at me. My pastor said that he was going to give an alter call for people to leave the church. It was heartbreaking to hear. The fear of being rejected came on me.

The devil immediately said to me, "Your pastor is talking about you and your crazy family. Get out!"

The Holy Spirit said to me loud and clear, "That statement made was not from Father God. It was the flesh side of your pastor, out of some sort of frustration at the time. You are not going anywhere."

The Holy Spirit shared with me that He would show me who was going to leave, and those that left needed to leave. The Holy Spirit said that some were going to leave to fulfill the purpose and assignment He had for them, some because their motives weren't right, some because of greed and the love of money, and some because they were loyal to man and not Father God.

The Holy Spirit said, "Those that leave for the love of money only see my children as gold mines. They are looking at the fruit of what's been a long journey of sacrifices I had your pastors to make on the behalf of me. Sherrie, you are not to give up. I need you to pray and keep your heart right. Because of this separation, the devil will cause division, doubt, fear, loyalty, and a sense to defend and a sense of defeat. None of this is from Father God. Some that left will return to our church. This is why I need you to keep your heart right, with no love lost for them."

The Holy Spirit shared that where Father God was taking my pastors there had to be a shift. For several months it was hard because some of those that left were people I had a personal impartation with and helped me during some difficult times. Every time I ran into someone who left the church, they tried to convince me to leave. The Holy Spirit always spoke to me and said, "No!" What I came to understand was that no matter who left me, God would never leave or stop the plan He had for me.

Another occasion at church I heard the Holy Spirit's instructions. I was dealing with sleepless nights and taking medication. Even with the medication I wasn't sleeping. My pastor did an alter call for people taking medication to sleep, for anxiety, for depression, and so much more. I had medication for each in my purse. I felt ashamed because everything my pastor mentioned I was taking. I heard the Holy Spirit loud and clear to go up to the alter and drop those medications there. I didn't want to be the first one, but I heard the Holy Spirit say move. As I moved, many others went up to the front. My pastor shared Proverbs 3:24: "When thou liest down, thou shalt not be afraid: yea, thou shalt lie down, and thy sleep shall be sweet." The Holy Spirit told me that from then on, when I got in my bed, my sleep would be deep and peaceful. Now, I laugh at my husband often because I can't stay up to watch a movie in bed with him. When I found a good movie, within 10 minutes, I'm sleep. One day, I hope he gets it that we need to watch the movies in the family room. The bedroom is off limits for movie watching with me.

The Holy Spirit has helped me with the simple things in life as well. One night, I came home from the grocery store and as we were bringing the bags in the house, I discovered that I lost my keys. I looked everywhere. While we were outside, I thought I left them in the door, and someone may have grabbed them. For four hours I looked for my keys. I finally called a locksmith to come and change our locks. While waiting on the locksmith, I began to pray and ask the Holy Spirit to help me find my keys. Immediately the Holy Spirit said to look behind the microwave.

"When you put the bags down, the keys fell behind it."

Just as the Holy Spirit spoke, I found my keys.

Another occasion, I misplaced my keys. While leaving out in the morning to head to work at 5, I couldn't find them. I was running 30 minutes behind. I began to pray and asked the Holy Spirit to help.

"Look down at the mailbox."

The mailbox was about 50 feet from my home. I left my keys dangling from the mailbox overnight. My house keys and car keys were on the chain. I thank God that nothing was missing or broken into. The Holy Spirit constantly talks to me and helps me to put my trust in God. Throughout the day in the workplace, the Holy Spirit is there to remind me that no matter who's against me, to continue to work unto the Lord. I've watched how God vindicated me when I was being accused and lied on. I felt like I needed to look for another job. The Holy Spirit reminded me that increase and promotion come from God, not man, and every door that He opened, only He can close it. I had to learn that by prematurely jumping out of fear I wasn't giving God time to vindicate, defend, or protect me. The Holy Spirit reminded me about James

1:12 (KJV), which read, "Blessed is the man that endured temptation for when he is tried, he shall receive the crown of life, which the Lord hath promised to them that love Him," and Psalm 9:9 (KJV), "The Lord is also will be a refuge for the oppressed, a refuge in the times of trouble."

I called out the names of those that were falsely accusing me of something I didn't do. I began to say out loud to God you are bigger than each name.

"God you are bigger than the position they have in this company. God you are bigger than this company. God your Word in Isaiah 54:17 (NIV) says, 'No weapon forged against you will prevail, and you will refute every tongue that accuses you. This is the heritage of the servants of the Lord, and this is their vindication from me,' declares the LORD."

I went into the bathroom at work to pray, confess Isaiah 54:17 and Psalm 91 whenever I felt afraid because too many people were coming against me. I began to speak 2 Timothy 1:7 (NKJV), "For God has not given us a spirit of fear, but of power and of love and of a sound mind." People who I thought would speak up on my behalf because they knew the accusations were not true didn't speak up. I had to go into prayer and find God's Word concerning even those that wouldn't speak up on my behalf. God gave me Romans 8:31-39 (NKJV):

"What then shall we say to these things? If God *is* for us, who *can be* against us? He who didn't spare His own Son, but delivered Him up for us all, how shall He not with Him also freely give us all things? Who shall bring a charge against God's elect? *It is* God who justifies. Who *is* he who condemns? *It is* Christ who died, and furthermore is also risen, who is even at the right hand of God, who also makes intercession for us. Who shall separate us from the love of Christ? *Shall* tribulation, or distress, or persecution, or famine, or nakedness, or peril, or sword? As it is written: "For Your sake we are killed all day long; We are accounted as sheep for the slaughter." Yet in all these things we are more than conquerors through Him who loved us. For I am persuaded that neither death nor life, nor angels nor principalities nor powers, nor things present nor things to come, nor height nor depth, nor any other created thing, shall be able to separate us from the love of God which is in Christ Jesus our Lord."

With every wrongful accusation in the workplace, as hard as it was, I knew God was going to vindicate me. I constantly heard the Holy Spirit tell me to trust God, continue to work unto the Lord, and keep my heart right. Those individuals that falsely accused me began to self-destruct. I thank God that He is my source, and those places of employment were resources given to me by Him.

The Holy Spirit helped me not to commit an affair when I worked in another city. It was a good opportunity and I needed time away from everyone. All hell was breaking loose in my life again. My daughter left to live with strangers I didn't know. My husband and I were dealing with conviction to change our way of living. My husband didn't move with me. I went home every Friday and went back in the early morning hours on Monday. I had my own studio apartment, and it was beautiful. I had a nice queen-size bedroom, tailored just for me. I did go to church on Sunday's during visits back home on the weekend. After work, I regularly walked the city for hours, not realizing I was losing weight. I went from a size 18 to a size 12. I worked at several law firms over my career, but hadn't worked around so many attractive good-looking men, from the mailroom to the managing partner. I saw six-packs abs and biceps, all day long. I hadn't dated a white man, but baby, those thoughts came across my mind. I wasn't a saint, but one thing in my heart that I didn't want God to call me out on since giving my life to

Him was adultery. I asked the Holy Spirit about those feelings and desires I was having.

One attorney was handsome. He wore tight-fitting polo shirts often, and when he wore a suit, most of the time his shirt was opened. His body was fit! He had the most beautiful eyes. He often came into the catering kitchen where I worked but didn't say anything. He just nodded his head while smiling. My heart melted. I called on the name of Jesus several times throughout the day when I saw him. He didn't come on to me or disrespect me in any way. I was the one having those desires and feelings. One night, I went straight to my studio and began to pray. I prayed to God to take away all desires or feelings about being attracted to other men besides my husband. I began to sob and thank God in advance that I was free. The next day, the attorney and I had a conversation. It was a good chat. I realized that he wasn't thinking about me or any other woman. The devil tried to tempt me with another attractive man, but that time the Holy Spirit used a simple but funny example to remind me I was married. I began to enjoy living in the other city and started staying over the weekend without going home on Fridays to be with my husband or going to church.

The Holy Spirit said to me, "Why you are willing to give up your big gulp with free refills to go after that six pack!"

One evening, the Holy Spirit was prompting me to go to my studio after work. I planned to go to dinner after work with someone. The Holy Spirit kept telling me all day to cancel the dinner and go to my studio. I cancelled dinner and went to my studio. When I opened my studio door, my husband was there to surprise me. He came from Maryland where we lived. I did go to dinner, and it was with my husband. We had a lovely evening. The Holy Spirit helped and guided me when I listened. Months later, I was instructed by the Holy Spirit to return home with my husband in Maryland and find another job in Washington, D.C. God made provisions and I was able to quickly find work. My husband's fear and worry were lifted off him. Truly, it wasn't about my husband. It was about my relationship with God. John 14:26 states, "But the Advocate, the Holy Spirit, whom the Father will send in my name, will teach you all things and will remind you of everything I have said to you."

-

Listen to that still small but loud voice in your heart. It is God speaking to you. Cast down imaginations that set you up for failure. The Spirit will bear witness with you. Romans 8:16 (KJV), reads, "The Spirit itself beareth witness with our spirit, that we are the children of God." Walk and not faint. Isaiah 40:31 (KJV) declares, "They that wait upon the Lord shall renew their strength, they shall mount up with wings as eagles; they shall run and not be weary, and they shall walk and not faint." The Holy Spirit is our helper sent by God until Jesus' second coming. Invite the Holy Spirit into your life. God sent Him. The Holy Spirit is great to talk to about anything. Before you make a move, seek the counsel of He, Him, Holy Spirit. The Holy Spirit even will bring laughter to your heart.

Chapter 18

SCRIPTURES TAILOR-MADE JUST FOR ME AND YOU

"For God so loved the world, that he gave his only begotten Son, that whosoever believeth in him should not perish, but have everlasting life."

- John 3:16 (KJV)

"Blessed *are* those who hunger and thirst for righteousness, For they shall be filled."

- Matthew 5:6 (NKJV)

"But seek first the kingdom of God and His righteousness, and all these things shall be added to you."

- Matthew 6:33 (NKJV)

I used these Scriptures to overcome my past and accept my new walk with Christ. I was able to accept the love, protection, and peace from God from the following Scriptures:

"But without faith *it is* impossible to please *Him*, for he who comes to God must believe that He is, and *that* He is a rewarder of those who diligently seek Him." - Hebrews 11:6 (NKJV)

"There is therefore now no condemnation to them which are in Christ Jesus, who walk not after the flesh, but after the Spirit. For the law of the Spirit of life in Christ Jesus hath made me free from the law of sin and death. For what the law couldn't do, in that it was weak through the flesh, God sending his own Son in the likeness of sinful flesh, and for sin, condemned sin in the flesh: That the righteousness of the law might be fulfilled in us, who walk not after the flesh, but after the Spirit. For they that are after the flesh do mind the things of the flesh; but they that are after the Spirit the things of the Spirit. For to be carnally minded is death; but to be spiritually minded is life and peace. Because the carnal mind is enmity against God: for it is not subject to the law of God, neither indeed can be. So then they that are in the flesh cannot please God. But ye are not in the flesh, but in the Spirit, if so be that the Spirit of God dwell in you. Now if any man have not the Spirit of Christ, he is none of his. And if Christ be in you, the body is dead because of sin; but the Spirit is life because of righteousness. But if the Spirit of him that raised up Jesus from the dead dwell in you, he that raised up Christ from the dead shall also quicken your mortal bodies by his Spirit that dwelleth in you. Therefore, brethren, we are debtors, not to the flesh, to live after the flesh. For if ye live after the flesh, ye shall die: but if ye through the Spirit do mortify the deeds of the body, ye shall live. For as many as are led by the Spirit of God, they are the sons of God. For ye have not received the spirit of bondage again to fear; but ye have received the Spirit of adoption, whereby we cry, Abba, Father. The Spirit itself beareth witness with our spirit, that we are the children of God: And if children, then heirs; heirs of God, and joint-heirs with Christ; if so be that we suffer with him, that we may be also glorified together. For I reckon that the sufferings of this present time are not worthy to be compared with the glory which shall be revealed in us. For the earnest expectation of the creature waiteth for the manifestation of the sons of God. For the creature was made subject to vanity, not willingly, but by reason of him who hath subjected the same in hope, Because the creature itself also shall be delivered from the bondage of corruption into the glorious liberty of the children of God. For we know that the whole creation groaneth and travaileth in pain together until now. And not only they, but ourselves also, which have the first fruits of the Spirit, even we ourselves groan within ourselves, waiting for the adoption, to wit, the redemption of our body. For we are saved by hope: but hope that is seen is not hope: for what a man seeth, why doth he yet hope for? But if we hope for that we see not, then do we with patience wait for it. Likewise the Spirit also helpeth our infirmities: for we know not what we should pray for as we ought: but the Spirit itself maketh intercession for us with groanings which cannot be uttered. And he that searcheth the hearts knoweth what is the mind of the Spirit, because he maketh intercession for the saints according to the will of God. And we know that all things work together for good to them that love God, to them who are the called according to his purpose. For whom he did foreknow, he also did predestinate to be conformed to the image of his Son, that he might be the firstborn among many brethren. Moreover whom he did predestinate, them he also called: and whom he called, them he also justified: and whom he justified, them he also glorified. What shall we then say to these things? If God be for us, who can be against us? He that spared not his own Son, but delivered him up for us all, how shall he not with him also freely give us all things? Who shall lay anything to the charge of God's elect? It is God that justifieth. Who is he that condemneth? It is Christ that died, yea rather, that is risen again, who is even at the right hand of God, who also maketh intercession for us. Who shall separate us from the love of Christ? shall tribulation, or distress, or persecution, or famine, or nakedness, or peril, or sword? As it is written, For thy sake we are killed all the day long; we are accounted as sheep for the slaughter. Nay, in all these things we are more than conquerors through him that loved us. For I am persuaded, that neither death, nor life, nor angels, nor principalities, nor powers, nor things present, nor things to come, Nor height, nor depth, nor any other creature, shall be able to separate us from the love of God, which is in Christ Jesus our Lord." - Romans 8 (KJV)

"He that dwelleth in the secret place of the most High shall abide under the shadow of the Almighty. I will say of the LORD, He is my refuge and my fortress: my God; in him will I trust. Surely he shall deliver thee from the snare of the fowler, and from the noisome pestilence. He shall cover thee with his feathers, and under his wings shalt thou trust: his truth shall be thy shield and buckler. Thou shalt not be afraid for the terror by night; nor for the arrow that flieth by day; Nor for the pestilence that walketh in darkness; nor for the destruction that wasteth at noonday. A thousand shall fall at thy side, and ten thousand at thy right hand; but it shall not come nigh thee. Only with thine eyes shalt thou behold and see the reward of the wicked. Because thou hast made the LORD, which is my refuge, even the most High, thy habitation; There shall no evil befall thee, neither shall any plague come nigh thy dwelling. For he shall give his angels charge over thee, to keep thee in all thy ways. They shall bear thee up in their hands, lest thou dash thy foot against a stone. Thou shalt tread upon the lion and adder: the young lion and the dragon shalt thou trample under feet. Because he hath set his love upon me, therefore will I deliver him: I will set him on high, because he hath known my name. He shall call upon me, and I will answer him: I will be with him in trouble; I will deliver him, and honour him. With long life will I satisfy him, and shew him my salvation." - Psalm 91 (KJV)

"For I know the thoughts that I think toward you, saith the Lord, thoughts of peace, and not of evil, to give you an expected end." - Jeremiah 29:11 (KJV)

"But ye shall receive power, after that the Holy Ghost is come upon you: and ye shall be witnesses unto me both in Jerusalem, and in all Judaea, and in Samaria, and unto the uttermost part of the earth." - Acts 1:8 (KJV)

"My soul followeth hard after thee: thy right hand upholdeth me. But those that seek my soul, to destroy it, shall go into the lower parts of the earth." - Psalm 63:8-9 (KJV)

"Therefore I tell you, do not worry about your life, what you will eat or drink; or about your body, what you will wear. Is not life more than food, and the body more than clothes? Look at the birds of the air; they do not sow or reap or store away in barns, and yet your heavenly Father feeds them. Are you not much more valuable than they? Can any one of you by worrying add a single hour to your life." - Matthew 6:25-27 (NIV)

"Confess your faults one to another, and pray one for another, that ye may be healed. The effectual fervent prayer of a righteous man availeth much." - James 5:16 (KJV)

"Delight yourself also in the Lord, And He shall give you the desires of your heart." - Psalm 37:4 (NKJV)

"Surely God is my salvation; I will trust and not be afraid. The Lord, the Lord himself, is my strength and my defense; he has become my salvation." - Isaiah 12:2 (NIV)

"I praise you because I am fearfully and wonderfully made; your works are wonderful, I know that full well." - Psalm 139:14 (NIV)

"And the peace of God, which transcends all understanding, will guard your hearts and your minds in Christ Jesus." - Philippians 4:7 (NIV)

"Take delight in the LORD, and he will give you the desires of your heart." - Psalm 37:4

"Trust in the LORD with all your heart, And lean not on your own understanding; In all your ways acknowledge Him, And He shall direct your paths." - Proverbs 3:5-6 (NKJV)

"being confident of this very thing, that He who has begun a good work in you will complete *it* until the day of Jesus Christ;" - Philippians 1:6 (NKJV)

The Bible was written for the Believer in Christ!

Chapter 19

UNTORTURED: WHERE I AM TODAY

"Before I formed thee in the belly I knew thee; and before thou calmest forth out of the womb I sanctified thee, and I ordained thee a prophet unto the nations!"

- Jeremiah 1:5

I thank my Heavenly Father that my past does not define my future! I'm a living witness that no matter what happens to us here on earth, if you are alive to share the victories God has brought you through, your past is only to help others get through. I truly accepted who I am and the love of God through Jesus daily. The devil had it out for me from day one, but my God! Being *untortured* today in my life reminds me to encourage others to keep going. You may have had a painful start, but it doesn't have to continue. We all have something that could have knocked the wind out of us, but if you have gotten passed it, you have won. The bruises with heal over time.

It's a constant daily effort to think on things that are mentioned in Philippians 4:8 (KJV): "Finally, brethren, whatsoever things are true, whatsoever things are honest, whatsoever things are just, whatsoever things are pure, whatsoever things are lovely, whatsoever things are of good report; if there be any virtue, and if there be any praise, think on these things. I'm constantly reviewing my thoughts and the thoughts that once tortured my mind. I make an effort to cast down imaginations as instructed in 2 Corinthians 10:3-6 (KJV): "For though we walk in the flesh, we don't war after the flesh: (For the weapons of our warfare are not carnal, but mighty through God to the pulling down of strong holds;) Casting down imaginations, and every high thing that exalteth itself against the knowledge of God, and bringing into captivity every thought to the obedience of Christ; And having in a readiness to revenge all disobedience, when your obedience is fulfilled."

One of the ways I have joy every day is that I get up with a thankful heart. I thank God the minute I open my eyes. No matter what's going on, I have thanksgiving at the front of every day. I make a constant effort to thank God for so many things we normally take for granted. I thank God for the use of my body, my functioning organs, the air I breathe, my family, even for the ones who get on my nerves, my husband, and a better relationship with daughter. I appreciate that I still have my mom to enjoy. I have all of my brother and sisters. I thank God for my in-laws. I thank God they are loving and kind towards me. I thank God for my nieces and nephews, they are special to me. My thankful list can go on and on. I love doing things I hadn't taken the time to enjoy like flowers in my home, going to the ballet and opera, looking up in the sky for no reason, and eating off my fine dinnerware. I love sharing the love of God with everyone, no matter who they are. It brings me so much joy.

I only became sane because of the love of Jesus in my life. Giving my life to Christ was the best thing I've ever done! Loving and learning with the help of the Holy Spirit has caused me to beat every attack from the devil. Even when the outcome wasn't what I expected it to be, I still sought the good in it and was thankful for the fact that I got through it.

I appreciate my husband. He played major part in my healing. In spite of our ups and downs and breaking free from behaviors we had that didn't bring glory to God, my husband didn't quit on me. He stayed. I learned over the years that I can only be mad at him from the neck up! Only married people will understand this! I watched my husband hunger after a relationship with God and beat the many odds against him. I watched how he lost everything and had nothing, but still held onto his vision and dreams, He let me know that we were going to be okay. The Holy Spirit reminds me about the good my husband has provided for me and to pay attention to the small love that I sometimes overlook.

My relationship with my daughter continues to evolve to new levels of love and understanding. I love how she respectfully expresses herself. She also willingly tries to get understanding. I'm grateful to see her excel in life and become an amazing woman. For my babies that are now present with the Lord, I truly believe I will hold them in heaven. I thank God for giving me another chance to love and care for other children.

Forgiveness is always at the forefront in my life. Everyone deserves another chance, no matter the offense. I'm learning to forgive when others asked with a sincere heart. Even if they don't apologize, my heart is fixed on forgiving everyone. Lamentations 3:22 (NIV) states, "Because of the Lord's great love we are not consumed, for his compassions never fail." I'm one conversation away from restoration with some people in my life. I didn't mean to hurt them, but more than anything, I know they didn't mean to hurt me either. My heart is fixed on the love of God. I love the clean heart I asked for. In Psalm 51:10 (KJV) it says, "Create in me a clean heart, O God; and renew a right spirit within me."

I wear lipstick and I take the pictures. I love me! For years, I didn't love me or even think that I could be loved.

I'm able to look in the mirror and love who I see. I have embraced the woman I see. For years I was bound by those awful words spoken over my life that I wasn't good enough, I was ugly, I was too skinny. I'm no longer ruled by them! I wear the lipstick and I take the pictures!

Jump!

One of my dearest friends I met through her husband laughed when she called him at work. She often heard me fussing him out and him calling me crazy! Whenever I came into their store, she laughed at something I said or did. She started calling me Comedienne ReeRee. She loved to post pictures on their store website and social media page. Whenever we took a picture, she let everyone know I was comedienne. In her honor after her untimely transition to heaven, which I was devastated, I gave stand-up comedy a try. I could hear her voice cheering me on each time. I jumped out there, scared to do what I always want to do. I had the best time ever, even though I sucked at it on most of the open mic nights! I had so much fun and met many wonderful people. That *jump* even gave me a chance to be on television! Over 1.8K viewers saw it on an online video format. I was nervous and couldn't speak. The news spokesman nicely put me on the spot on the set on national television. I was frozen solid. The segment was aired for about 10 minutes. Only a select few in the industry could get on that platform, which had a waiting list. God opened that door for me with my inexperienced self. I spoke to one of my brothers in Christ after church service. I shared how I believed I didn't do well on the set. He blessed me with some valuable knowledge.

He said, "Most people in the beginning worry about the performance which is the least. This is how it should be in the beginning...60% is the exposure, 30% is image, and 10% is the performance. Sister, you were exposed to something good. Over time, the performance will get better. Keep going." Thank brother Henry Armstrong for that input and for encouraging me with your advice. His advice helped me to keep going. The invitation came from someone who took me under her wing and allowed me to be with her on several of her shows. I had backstage passes too. Our connection came through that dear friend who loved us both. Thank you LaShawn Lindsey, may you continue to rest in heaven until we meet again. Queen Aishah, thank you for taking me under your wing in comedy. I had an amazing time.

What was so good about my jump was that it gave me the confidence to speak in front of people and try several open mic nights. Many seasoned comedians cheered me on during each try. I'm turning my testimony into a laugh-a-mony! As I move forward into my future and all that God has for me, I'm excited to know that I can began again. I will jump again from the same cliff! Wait and watch!

-

My dear readers, you can begin again! Your latter will be greater! Keep moving with Jesus! Just know that according to Philippians 1:6, "...He who has begun a good work in you will complete *it* until the day of Jesus Christ;" (Philippians 1:6 (NKJV)). You'll be surprised with what's ahead of you! Forgive, love, and receive love! The just shall live by faith. "Then the LORD answered me and said: "Write the vision and make it plain on tablets, that he may run who reads it," states Habakkuk 2:2 (NKJV). Philippians 3:13-14 reads, "Brethren, I count not myself to have apprehended: but this one thing I do, forgetting those things which are behind, and reaching forth unto those things which are before, I press toward the mark for the prize of the high calling of God in Christ Jesus."

About the Author

Sherry Ann Walker is a faithful Christian and a proud wife and mother. Faith and family are most important to her. She attended Anacostia Senior High School where she was a varsity cheerleader. These days, Sherry is a cheerleader for Jesus Christ. She relentlessly cheers for love and acceptance for all mankind.

In her spare time, Sherry enjoys comedy. Naturally funny and a good storyteller, she started her comedic career and performed at open-mic nights for a while. She truly believes that good humor and laughter feeds and rejuvenates the soul and contributes to good health. Sherry took a brief hiatus from comedy to concentrate on her first book. She has plans to resume open-mic nights in near the future. Sherry is also an amazing interior designer and loves decorating homes. She is happiest when spending time with her family and friends and fellowshipping with other women. Sherry truly believes women could unify the world by coming together with their hearts and minds and utilizing the talents and gifts God has given them.

Sherry Ann Walker resides in the Washington, D.C. metropolitan area.

Contact

If you wish for Sherry Walker to participate in speaking engagements, please send an email to untortured2021@gmail.com.